FREEDOM, FASCISTS, FOOLS, & FRAUDS:

Bapton Books Position Papers and Other
Critical Pieces, 2011 - 2014

Gervase MW Wemyss
Markham Shaw Pyle

Bapton Books

Markham Shaw Pyle, author of *"Fools, Drunks, and the United States": August 12 1941,* and of *Benevolent Designs: The Countess and the General: George Washington, Selina Countess of Huntingdon, their correspondence, & the evangelizing of America,* holds his undergraduate and law degrees from Washington & Lee. He is a past or current member of, inter alia, the Organization of American Historians; the Society for Military History; the Southern Historical Association; the Southwestern Social Science Association; the Southwestern Historical Association; the Southwestern Political Science Association; the Virginia Historical Society; and the Texas State Historical Association. He is the co-author of *The Transatlantic Disputations: Essays & Observations; The Bapton Books Sampler: a literary chrestomathy;* and *When That Great Ship Went Down: the legal and political repercussions of the loss of RMS* Titanic; and co-editor and co-annotator of *The Complete Mowgli Stories, Duly Annotated,* and *The Annotated* Wind in the Willows, *for Adults and Sensible Children (or, possibly, Children and Sensible Adults).*

GMW Wemyss lives and writes, wisely pseudonymously, in Wilts. Having, by invoking the protective colouration of tweeds, cricket (he was a dry bob at school), and country matters, somehow evaded immersion in Mercury whilst up at University, he survived to become the author of *Cross and Poppy: a village tale; The 1940* and of *Sensible Places: essays* *Confidence of the House: May on time, place & countryside;* co-author of *The Transatlantic Observation; The Bapton Books* *Disputations: Essays & Sampler: a literary chrestomathy;* and *When That Great Ship Went Down: the legal and political repercussions of the loss of RMS* Titanic; and co-editor and co-annotator of *The Complete Mowgli Stories, Duly Annotated,* and *The Annotated* Wind in the Willows, *for Adults and Sensible Children (or, possibly, Children and Sensible Adults).*

Together, they are the partners in Bapton Books.

A note to the reader: it is the aspiration of this imprint, small though Bapton Books be, to have as few errors and literals – 'typographical errors', misprints – as occur in any average Oxford University Press publication (which, alas, in these thin and piping times, gives us a margin of perhaps five or ten). Any obliging corrections shall be gratefully received.

FREEDOM, FASCISTS, FOOLS, & FRAUDS:

Bapton Books Position Papers and Other Critical Pieces, 2011 - 2014

Gervase MW Wemyss
Markham Shaw Pyle

BAPTON BOOKS

CONTENTS:

A word in your shell-like:

Y ou'll see us saying, a bit later on, that Cassandra —doomed to prophesy truth, to be ignored, and to be proved painfully and bitterly right —may well have been the first writer.

We have collected here analyses, including past Bapton Books Position Papers, from the past few years, on matters of import, or portent, or which were straws in the wind. In looking back over these few years' worth of analysis, it strikes us —quite depressingly —that we were all too prescient: save that we were all too optimistic.

Even as this volume went to press, there were yet further assaults on freedom —notably including freedom of speech, of expression, and of publication —and yet more examples of cowardice, political and otherwise, that allow the private opponents of freedom to metastasise into *State* persecutors of dissent.

If we have two themes here —and we do, because events have forced us to do, to concentrate upon these two themes of many that we might have chosen —they are the totalitarian itch as expressed domestically and in foreign affairs alike, from invasions of territory to invasions of the bounds of free speech and freedom of thought; and the cowardice or collaboration, the appeasement and the acquiescence, that enables and emboldens these.

And we *have* collected here these previous Bapton Books position papers and other analyses and, yes, polemics, for two reasons: for ease of reference, and because these insights (being, alas, all too prescient) are of use in understanding how we in the West came to the present sorry pass. We regret only that we were far too often spot-on.

That was the news of the week that was in the world:
11 July 2011 - and it merely got worse...

This piece was written at the very beginning of the latest 'long, downward slurge': before the threat of Leveson was abroad in the land or troughing, expenses-fiddling politicians seized upon it – in the name, of course, of protecting the Little People from being, ever, in any way offended or made unhappy – as a means of controlling a free press and evading scrutiny. Mr Wemyss is saddened beyond measure that what he discerned was not *a mirage. Even then, it was possible to discern the appalling outlines of what might befall: no expenses investigations ever again; no exposure of a future Jimmy Savile; no justice for another Hillsborough.... All the same, Mr Wemyss shan't pretend he ever imagined, in his most dour and depressive moments, what has come of it since.*

It has been a curious week. I am now returned from a (in most senses) happy retreat into the purer world of cricket, although the 'Varsity match was in its actual *result* not calculated to please me; and I find all changed, changed utterly. In fact, change and decay in all around I see.

There is sadness, but no sense that the times are out of joint, at the news that Josef Suk the Younger has died, laden with years and achievement: this is in the natural order of things, and that Antonín Dvořák's great-grandson should have been so long amongst us is simply an uncovenanted grace, the passing of which one cannot claim as a cutting short.

Other items in the week's budget of news, however, are neither timely nor natural.

That *The News of the World* deserved to go under is unquestioned and unquestionable: the market spoke, and that is that —and quite right, too. That this was an ignominious end for a newspaper that, over a century and a half, has done much good along with much bad, is also beyond cavil. That the party leaders are dabbling in its gore, however, is ominous in the extreme.

It is quite true that the PCC does not emerge from this episode covered with glory; no more does PC Plod. It is imperative, however, to note that it was news reporting, by the unlikely team of the *Grauniad* and *The Torygraph,* that led to the mass revulsion that expressed itself, through the market, in demanding that *The News of the Screws* cease to be.

Yet what dangers now inhere in what comes after.

The Prime Minister had, as we all know, hired Mr Andrew Coulson, late of *The News of the World,* as director of communications, first for the Party and then for the PM. It is not illegitimate for his political rivals to question his judgement in consequence; it is equally legitimate for the PM to say, He believed in the concepts of redemption and the second chance, and he believed Mr Coulson's protestations that he had not been personally guilty of the sins of his organisation. I hold no brief for the Prime Minister or his tendency —I had almost said, his faction —within the Conservative Party; yet I should prefer not to live in a world in which no one believed in second chances. That sort of grim Calvinism is not for me, congenial as it may be to certain elements in all parties, Labour and the Liberal Democrats not least.

What is wholly illegitimate is the way in which the political class has seized upon this in hopes of reducing the liberty of the subject.

Were I to meet my Maker this night —an ordeal for which I think neither of us is altogether prepared, to paraphrase the Great Man —I should have little enough to show for myself. That is why I don't care for the idea that there are no second chances: I am evidently not as Practically Perfect in Every Way as the sainted moralists now lecturing us, such as Mr Huhne (ahem). I could however at least point with a craftsman's pride to my account of the fall of the Chamberlain government and the emergence of Churchill as PM in our darkest hour. And, speaking as one who has some knowledge of the subject, I must tell you that the current crop of professional politicians —men and women who have never been or done anything with their lives save to essay the long climb of the greasy pole (and who, unlike Dizzy, could no more have coined that phrase than could one of my Gloucester Old Spots); men and women whose ascent of the greasy pole is not even for any purpose of enacting their principles, but is rather the pole-dancing of whores looking for a few quid to be tucked into their exiguous garments by the punters —I must tell you that the current crop of professional politicians are not fit to be mentioned in the same breath as the hon. and right hon. Members of May 1940. Of course there is no Churchill today, nor Amery, nor Keyes, nor any Commander Bower; there is no Clem, no Arthur Greenwood, no Josiah Wedgwood; and there is assuredly no Archie Sinclair on the Lib Dem benches. But there is likewise no Geoffrey Mander on the backbenches, no man of parts of the George Hicks stamp, no Sir Joseph Nall. The average hon. Member of today, the average right hon. Member of today, is a creature without bowels or breeding, with no moral or intellectual hinterland, evolutionarily adapted only to a tiny zone within Westminster, and wholly innocent of any conception of common life and common liberty.

They are the creatures who blagged their expenses; will *not* be weaned from the public teat; plunder the public fisc without blinking; bully their staffs —and exercise *droit de seigneur* over the more fanciable of them, when they can; even now resent the idea that their expenses should be examined or reported to their constituencies; and regard the public, and the public purse, as a vast, complaisant milch-cow. Or Bercow.

And in the wake of the scandal engulfing one tabloid, they are seized with, and of, the unholy, gleeful idea of seizing control of the press. It were, after all, so much more convenient that the press be muzzled. No more investigations; no more exposures of porno channels, moats, and duck houses; no more impertinent questions from those who don't know their place, damn it all, about bung or bribes or buggery or driving licences....

They mustn't be allowed to do this.

Journalism is a grubby business —almost as grubby as politics. The inky wretches who have engaged in the trade are a rag-tag lot: Churchill and Orwell, Addison and Johnson, Kipling and Chesterton. Yet it is history in a hurry, and it is more fundamentally honest than the politicians' hunt for tufts and place and preferment; and it contains its own corrective —as witness the exposure of the present scandal *by other newspapers* —and is the sole corrective and check upon the politicians.

Journalism is a grubby business —almost as grubby as politics. And *The News of the Screws* —which, as that bye-name suggests, was read as avidly by barristers (and, if Miss Sayers is to be believed, by gentleman-detectives) for its modern Newgate Calendar as it was by punters seeking titillation (or simply tits) —was always grubby. It was as grubby as *The Cake* and *The Bun,* in Kipling's cautionary tale: and as useful in exposing corrupt JP-MPs and their flat-earth villages. Much of the current impetus to control the Press in the wake of this scandal is class-driven (and not least by Labour, which has long been alien to and contemptuous of actual labourers). Yet it is far worse than that, even, for it is the attempt of the professional political class to choke off any reporting of their misdeeds, forevermore, and to create an almost Soviet 'press'.

Not so very long ago, as Kleio views things, a group of expat Englishmen considered this problem, and set down that the government 'shall make no law ... abridging the freedom ... of the press'; and one of them said, wisely, that it was better for liberty to have newspapers without a government than a government without newspapers. That these expats were now become Americans is no reason not to repatriate those principles to this realm, for the principles were English, and derived from those events of 1689 that, whatever else one says of them, put paid at last to absolutism. And as if to vindicate those ideas in the land of their origin, the General Strike of 1926 stands as an example of their applicability.

The noisomely unseemly spectacle of the party leaders and their jackals seeking, in Rahm Emanuel's phrase, not to allow a crisis to go to waste, should stiffen the resolve of all who love liberty. Where crimes were committed, let them be prosecuted. But let's not pretend, and let us not allow the political classes, cosily closing ranks even as they engage in parliamentary kabuki, to pretend, that the solution is for the State to seize control over the Press: for that is a long step forward upon the road to serfdom. And Britons, after all —it is the charter of the land —shall never be slaves. Least of all to this sorry lot.

The dog of (culture) war and 'zero tolerance'

11 July 2012, and since

> *There is no word, perhaps, that frightens a politician more than does the word, 'accountability'; and the terror which that word inspires in politicians is as nothing to the bowel-loosening fear its utterance provokes in the tin-pot, fascist, tuft-hunting, unelected politicians we call 'bureaucrats' and 'civil servants' – who rarely remember that they are* servants, *not masters, and are* never civil *–, and 'Eurocrats' and 'quangocrats'. They are avid in looking out such devices as legal absolutism and 'zero tolerance', best praggers and guidelines, so as to avoid responsibility, accountability, and the making of decisions; and, having first flown from the terrors of liberty (and consequent responsibility) for themselves, then seek, like the tailless fox of the proverbs, to strip the rest of us of our* liberties. *By way of example, at once contemptible in itself and minatorily ominous in its implications, there is the appalling story of the killing of Lennox, the guiltless dog.*

On 11 July 2012, an inoffensive and innocent dog named Lennox was killed in Northern Ireland. Well, judicially murdered. Belfast Council and a —shall we say, less than credible —dog warden, one Alexandra Lightfoot, along with judicial officers who do not deserve to be numbered amongst HM judges, decided, on insufficient, dubious, and —shall we say, less than credible —evidence, that he was 'dangerous' and, although not a 'pit bull', was a '"pit bull" *type*'. They took refuge in the usual funkhole of legal absolutism and 'zero tolerance', and the other pretexts against thought and responsibility so beloved of fools, cowards, crooks, and bullies; whinged endlessly about how it was *they* who were being 'persecuted'; refused all appeals to sense, mercy, common decency, and compromise; engaged in gratuitous cruelty towards Lennox and the family who loved him (seeming to take malign pleasure in doing so, particularly as regarded the young daughter whose loving companion Lennox was); and generally conducted themselves as a peculiarly contemptible troop of trousered baboons. They spent, indeed, the majority of their efforts in attempting to silence public outcry, scrub opposing viewpoints from public discourse, retaliate against dissidents, and vindicate their own precious dignity of place and preferment.

They were, and are, utter shits.

Like all civilised, thinking humans (a category that excludes Belfast Council, its creatures, and the disgraces to the judiciary who were involved in this contemptible affair), Mr Pyle was, and remains, appalled and angry. Mr Wemyss went —and remains —well beyond mere anger and appal, and immediately published (in the comparatively free United States, through Mr Pyle's good graces) a few words:

To the abject and contemptible creatures
of Belfast Council,
Northern Ireland

Upon the occasion of the destruction of the dog, Lennox, and in the spirit of Yeats and GKC.

> When at last you're brought to answer
> At your God's eternal throne —
> Not for any creed you're cloaked in,

But your actions, all alone —
Do you think you'll be called faithful?
A just servant who's done well?
Or will God set Lennox on you,
For to harry you to Hell?

Perhaps the dog was Papist?
Or, perhaps, too much a Prod?
You're the scruff of Northern Ireland:
Don't pretend you have a God.
You are perjurers by lineage.
You were born to creep and crawl.
An embarrassment to all faiths:
Walking proof of mankind's Fall.

Your prayers are all for riches,
Your religion's just for show.
I shall laugh, you sons of bitches,
When the hellhounds bring you low.
You are Mother Ireland's bastards,
You are Ulster's lasting shame,
The spawn of scum and villain
Born of slatterns on the game.

Oh, your fat and bestial faces,
With free meals and gargle red,
They will pale in sudden horror
When you wake to know you're dead:
Those jowls so sleek with butter,
Flushed with whisky and long sin,
Will quiver like the blancmange
When God sees the state you're in;

He will whistle up archangels,
As the Master calls his whips,
And they'll loose the hounds of heaven
Who'll drain colour from your lips.
And Lennox will be granted,
Then, the justice you denied,

When Hunt and Host of justice
Drain the stirrup-cup, and ride:

Sure you'll not take any straight line —
As your life was, so your death —
You will jink and double backwards,
You will pant at last for breath:
And they'll hunt you from all Heaven
And across the hobs of Hell,
Because you ... you *politicians* ...
Had believed that you'd done well.

You: the scum of Northern Ireland,
Who presume to lobby God,
You whose piety is falsehood,
Each in fact but an Ould Sod:
You are perjurers by lineage.
You were born to creep and crawl.
An embarrassment to all faiths:
Walking proof of mankind's Fall.

You who kill the dogs of children —
(You'd steal corgis from the Queen) —
I suppose you'd kill a guide dog
And not think the deed obscene.
Hooker, Knox, or good St. Francis,
There is none to speak for you,
When the final Notes are called in
And your sins at last come due.

Your tarnished chains of office,
And your sashes, orange or vert:
Go, make them into nooses
And mete out your own desert.
Let the sobs of dogs and children
Be replaced with shouts of glee:
When you hang, as well you ought to,
On a bitter Judas tree.

There's a Wild Hunt over Ulster,
And the skies are full of dread,
For an awful Doom is given
And the just pronouncement read:
'Let the council who have chosen
'A disabled child to grieve
'By slaughtering her helper —
'And refusing all reprieve —

'Be rightly given over
'To their Master, down in Hell:
'Strike them from the rolls they sully;
'Let them aye in brimstone dwell.
'They have shamed their petty office,
'They have made their names as mud,
'And upon their crooked fingers
'Are the marks of guiltless blood.'

You are vile beyond description,
Petty tyrants of your land,
And have made the name of Belfast
For contempt and shame to stand.
Let your awful Doom be given
And the just pronouncement read:
'These buggers slaughtered Lennox.
'None shall weep when they are dead.'

May your road fall gaping from you,
May you reel to meet your fates;
May Cerberus in pieces
Rend you at the Devil's gates;
May you be the foxes' portion.
May your memories be damned.
You shall find in Hell your places.
We'd not see God's Heaven crammed.

As for Lennox and his owners,
They shall gambol in God's parks,
Whilst you writhe in fiery torment

As the guiltless Lennox barks.
Your howls, transformed to music,
Shall as sparks to Heaven fly.
Oh, it really doesn't matter:
Just you make it quick, and die.

Postscriptum: If you contemptible little people are so rash as to attempt to try to bring an action against poetry, just you try it on and see, God Almighty damn your shrivelled souls. Birkenhead was far too wise and learned in the law to sue Chesterton, and I strongly suggest you lot not show yourself even more vicious and contemptible than you are – were that possible.

It can come as no surprise that this sort of attitude has not been confined to the persecution by the overweening State (and Statist, Stasi-style weenies) of innocent animals. Thousands of children are tortured and indeed killed whilst —as in the case of Baby P —the Leftist, unionised jobsworths and jacks-in-office of the *soi-disant* social services, look on with expressions of bovine ignorance and disinterest; the secret family courts in the UK are a noisome scandal that should have raised eyebrows in the Third Reich; playgrounds are cleared because chilli peppers are found in a load of wood chips, children suffer frostbite in mindless drills, and students are expelled because another student with a history of bullying *accuses his usual victim* of twirling a pencil in his fingers and somehow doing so 'as if it were a gun'; and all the while, the pig-ignorant apparatchiki of the social services and the educationist establishment defend their actions and their refusal to *think* by resort to the same excuses of 'zero tolerance'. Meanwhile, they let their schools get shot up or allow mad knife-wielders to run amok in them whilst they waste time and public monies on things that no sane adult should think twice upon.

It's not only the dogs that are in danger from these fools, bullies, and cowards; it's the children as well. We are grimly delighted to expose these abjectly contemptible anthropoids, with their cow-college, plate-glass degrees, to the just execration of the public, as being at once instinctively fascist, unutterably stupid, and abysmally incompetent to run a whelk stall.

Free speech & its enemies:

22 October 2012 - and ever since

> *We've now seen the root of the problem, in one sense: the hatred of being questioned; the will to crush all dissent – and all dissenters; the determination, at all costs, to preserve one's place and position, preferment and pay-packet, privileges and emoluments; the abject cowardice when faced with the mere prospect of question or debate. We now look – in a piece published in the aftermath of Benghazi, and the outright lies and scapegoating in which* the United States government, **as a government,** indulged *—at what sour and ashen Dead Sea fruits these roots bear: how the denial of free speech as an all but absolute right, by private individuals and thence, inevitably, by the State, burgeons and disseminates, and what comes of this malignant growth – particularly when it is encouraged in the interest of a political position that brooks no dissent.*

Declaring an interest

We begin by Declaring an Interest. We are authors; and we are publishers. Free speech and freedom of the press and of publication, to the very outermost limits necessary to an orderly society under law, is our position, our livelihood, and our deepest principle.

It is utterly infuriating that we should be thus required to declare an interest; and it is simply contemptible that our so doing should seem in the least to suggest that this position and this principle is a function of our profession, rather than being the interest of every person on the planet save tyrants and their lackeys. Free speech, and freedom of the press and of publication as its corollary, to the very outermost limits necessary to an orderly society under law, *is an absolute human right possessed of everyone on this spinning globe, and ought to be the basic presumption and fiercely-defended birthright of each of us.*

A word about writers, artists, and other creators

Neither Hesiod nor Homer was the first writer; but Cassandra — impelled by divine decree to see and to speak, to be disbelieved, condemned, ignored, rebutted (*not* refuted), unheeded, and, in the end, dead right —may well have been.

Poets and sober historians, novelists and biographers —and visual artists, composers, and all those who are driven to create and to express —all alike share her doom, her *wyrd,* her fate.

Creative artists are odd creatures. Rarely do they stand at the head of affairs: Wilson was a very poor president; Jefferson's triumphs were less glorious than his defeats and failures were dark and contemptible; Disraeli fared rather better, but left little lasting monument; only Cicero and Churchill, the latter a painter as well as a writer, knew true triumph —and saw it slip irresistibly away into the defeat of what they most cherished and had striven to preserve. Writers especially believe that to have said or minuted a thing is to have done it, and their inner lives too often consume their lives in this world, leaving them to fail at the last amidst all the things they should have sworn they had *done,* but had only talked of doing and taken as having been accomplished.

All creative artists share Cassandra's doom, her *wyrd,* her fate. And all creative artists, like Cassandra, survive their times and their detractors, even if only as the fools and failures with whom greater artists quarrelled, and, in quarrelling and contest, made themselves great —and their foils, immortal.

All creative artists share Cassandra's doom, her *wyrd,* her fate: for all are *forced* to create, will they or nil they. In the last days of the final edits to this Paper, the authors have been, as so often before, reminded of this.

On the last eve of Summer, a friend of Mr Pyle's recalled to him an article Mr Pyle had written some three decades prior: one that Mr Pyle, after three decades, a breakdown or three in health, at least one seizure, and much more beside, no longer remembers, although he is gratified that it has *been* remembered. The article in its turn recalled to him another, which also he had written in his university days: which article he also but vaguely recalls, but the reaction to which has not left him. He and some friends had been sent to a conference at another university; and upon his return, Mr Pyle waxed humorous in print, to the displeasure of several of his acquaintance and of the professors who had despatched them to the conference: 'spitting on the decks', one of the professors called it. Perhaps it was. It ought to have been at that moment —although it wasn't, yet —that all concerned realised that Mr Pyle was always going to be an inky wretch, a scribbling writer: for the only response he could make then and can make now is Faulkner's, that '[t]he writer's only responsibility is to his art. He will be completely ruthless if he is a good one. He has a dream. It anguishes him so much that he can't get rid of it. He has no peace until then. Everything goes by the board: honor, pride, decency, security, happiness, all, to get the book written. If a writer has to rob his mother, he will not hesitate; the "Ode on a Grecian

Urn" is worth any number of old ladies.'

On the last eve of Summer, Mr Wemyss, pardonably gloating, announced to his friends that he was availing himself of an unexpected opportunity for a Dirty Weekend with a young man he'd recently met. Mr Pyle's sole comment was, 'Fine. Okay. That's why the revenues in this firm aren't a 50-50 split, neighbor. But I don't care if you're recreating the fall of Sodom with the whole Tottenham side, if I email you about these edits, pal, I expect a response. Have fun —but keep your phone handy and your PC on.' If Mr Pyle takes his text from Faulkner, it is Mr Wemyss' foible to take his from Wilde, perhaps the only true thing Oscar ever said: 'There is no such thing as a moral or immoral book. Books are either well written or badly written. That is all.'

On the morning of the first day of Autumn, Mr Pyle took his accustomed morning constitutional. There was a faint veil of ground-mist where a lawn ran happily away into a small wood, and another where a fence of palings enclosed another lawn; and although these things were not new, and never are, on the day of the autumnal equinox they are always and ever freighted with portent, and Mr Pyle, being an inky wretch of a writer, without thinking, marked them, and inevitably endured the irruption into his conscious mind of Keats' 'mists and mellow fruitfulness'. There were — on this first weekend of dove season —corvids about as well, black as a censor's heart and as big as original sin, thrice 'twa corbies', and, without thinking, Mr Pyle found himself asking them, 'Is Duncan not awake?'

He returned home to find that, in fact, a question about the edits had had its answer overnight, at what had been clearly the wee hours in the UK. A clearly (if happily) exhausted Mr Wemyss had written also this wry postscript: 'altho' having time of my life am finding self casting events as they occur into narrative prose for later use'.

This is life for writers and all creative artists. Friends and acquaintances (and, apparently, transient amours) find themselves made over into the raw material of art; persons who interact publicly with authors do so at their peril, as anecdotes in this Paper shall show. Writers literally cannot help themselves: there is that in them that helps itself to incident as at a buffet, piling the plate high. To attempt to censor this is not only wrong; it is foolish, and futile, and, in the end, doomed. Truth, like murder, *will* out, rather sooner than later. And because no two creative artists see the same thing, and neither sees what you see, and because they are compelled to show you what they have seen, it is a wicked disservice to humanity to attempt to suppress those visions. (It was, we seem to recall, Madeleine L'Engle who told the story of a writer's conference at an American state university which was running up a new building at the time. As three or so writers were passing by the floodlit construction site in the darkness, the poet amongst them turned rhapsode, noting the colours and textures of night and light, of materials and earths and machinery. At last she finished sharing her sudden glimpse of vision, and turned —perhaps a trifle condescendingly? —to the detective story writer, the author of mysteries, for his 'take' on the scene. He shrugged. 'Great place to hide a body,' said he.) Because no two creative artists see the same thing, and neither sees what you see, and because they are compelled to show you what they have seen, it is a wicked thing to attempt to suppress those visions: *and it is an utterly futile effort.* The creative impulse is unsleeping, and it cannot be repressed. Even in the events of the last few days of editing this Paper, it sprung forth; and even as Mr Wemyss, in, apparently, carnal ecstasy, had found himself evolving narrative prose to capture and recapture the moment after, in tranquillity, so also Mr Pyle, on his morning walk, noted his own responses *and his responses to his responses* to mist and corvidæ, knowing that these in turn should find their way into these notes.

For this is the point, at the end: the sharp, poignard point that inevitably, at the last, slips itself between the censor's ribs, to pierce his black and shrivelled heart. The censor and the murderous mob cannot stop the creative artist, for the creative artist cannot stop himself; and although one or another creator may be killed or daunted, that killing and that repression in itself furnishes material for creation by others: the creation of art that mocks the censor for all eternity, and is mockingly repeated to him in —*as* – the torments of the hell that censors deserve, and to which their desiccated souls go when they at last realise that they are, and have for years of seeming life been, dead as Marley, for all their vestments and parades of piety.

A word on usage

L amentably, in discussing free speech and its enemies, it shall be necessary —obviously —to refer, upon occasion, to instances of free speech that are quite likely to give maiden aunts of both sexes the vapours. Yet more lamentably, the enemies of free speech do include certain groups of people who have demonstrated a very thin skin indeed. As a matter of manners, one does attempt, so far as is possible, to designate people by their preferred terms of group self-identity. However, accuracy —Truth —is much more important even than are manners: *amicus Plato, sed magis amica veritas.*[1]

---

[1] As, indeed, Socrates himself is effectively made to say, in the *Phædo:* παρεσκευασμένος δή, ἔφη, ὦ Σιμμία τε καὶ Κέβης, οὑτωσὶ ἔρχομαι ἐπὶ τὸν λόγον: ὑμεῖς μέντοι, ἂν ἐμοὶ πείθησθε, σμικρὸν

Consequently, we shall call the Left as leftists, not 'liberals', for they are *not* Liberals. *We* are —which is why Mr Wemyss is perforce a member of the Conservative Party, it being the only major party in Britain with any room for Liberals (the problem with the Liberal Democrats is that, despite the presence of some quite decent Orange Bookers, it is neither Liberal nor democratic). Gladstone was a Liberal; as was Rosebery; as was indeed Hayek —and Burke (what did you *think* the Rockingham Whigs were?). Almost all of the 'Right' in America, although called 'conservatives', are classical Liberals, Mr Pyle very much included. The Left are illiberal in every way, always and everywhere the enemies of liberty, and ought not to be allowed to lie about it.

And, of course, we come next to Salafists and other Islamists, and to their ability to mobilise against free speech at least a significant part of the Muslim *ummah* —and to silence almost wholly the rest of that community, even if it be in fact a majority, which one hopes but cannot prove.[2]

The authors happen to be, both of them, members — extremely disaffected, because generally orthodox, members — of the Anglican Communion, or what's left of it. In any case, they are monotheists, because reason impels them to that conclusion, fond as they may be of the music of Rush. Both respect the right of all persons to hold what religious or irreligious or anti-religious views they choose, and to have those views, including atheism, tolerated *within reason*. ('Within reason': if some recent graduate of an Anglican theological seminary were, as is all too possible, to announce tomorrow his creation of the First Flower War Aztec Church,

---

φροντίσαντες Σωκράτους, τῆς δὲ ἀληθείας πολὺ μᾶλλον, ἐὰν μέν τι ὑμῖν δοκῶ ἀληθὲς λέγειν, συνομολογήσατε, εἰ δὲ μή, παντὶ λόγῳ ἀντιτείνετε, εὐλαβούμενοι ὅπως μὴ ἐγὼ ὑπὸ προθυμίας ἅμα ἐμαυτόν τε καὶ ὑμᾶς ἐξαπατήσας, ὥσπερ μέλιττα τὸ κέντρον ἐγκαταλιπὼν οἰχήσομαι.

[2] If they are, they want to stand up and be counted, this bloody minute: as they are doing in Libya.

with human sacrifices, or proclaim her becoming Priestess of Diana of the Ephesians, along with plans for temple prostitutes (under-aged ones at that), then the law should rightly step in and say, No: that is taking tolerance too far, not because we think it blasphemous, but because we, the People who comprise the State, do not permit this under any cloak or affected disguise.)

Toleration is not approval; it often does not, and it conceptually need not, imply respect, save for the principle of toleration itself. However, the authors are willing to respect the traditions of their neighbours, with the same caveat as before; and expect the same in return. Neither has any personal animus towards individual members of other faiths (indeed, Mr Wemyss' primary interactions with Muslims, Sikhs, and Hindus are focussed solely on their run rates when batting and their ability to take economical wickets whilst bowling). And it is precisely this respect that leads the authors to dispense with referring to Muhammad, the founder of Islam,[3] as a, or the, prophet. We do not expect Muslims or Jews to refer to Jesus as Christ, the Messiah, the Son of God, God the Son, the Second Person of the Trinity: a monotheist[4] who thus refers to him has a specific designation, and that designation is, 'Christian'. Similarly, as monotheists, the authors do not refer to Muhammad as a (or the) prophet, for to do so is,

---

[3] Presumably, and if he in fact existed and was thus named: a question of historicity that is not in fact settled – and which far too many people, no few of them armed and dangerous, believe ought not to be raised.

[4] Judaism, Christianity, and Islam all found their creedal statements upon the unity of the Deity. The *Shema* ends it there: 'Hear, O Israel: the Lord our God, the Lord is one'; the *shahada* declares the unity of the Deity and then asserts that Muhammad is his messenger; and of course, as people used to know, the Creed begins, *Credo in unum Deum,* 'I believe in one God, the Father Almighty, maker of Heaven and Earth', and goes on to profess belief in 'one Lord Jesus Christ, the only-begotten Son of God', in 'the Holy Ghost, The Lord and giver of life', and in 'one Catholick and Apostolick Church', 'one Baptism for the remission of sins', 'the Resurrection of the dead, and the life of the world to come'. It's really quite appalling that we want to remind people of this; if nothing else, those reading this paper, which is after all in English, ought really to be aware of the *literary* heritage founded upon Cranmer's prose and the *BCP*.

in effect, to recite the *shahada* and become a Muslim. Did either of the authors, believing as they do in one God, also regard Muhammad as the prophet of that God, and the revelations conventionally ascribed to him as true, intellectual honesty should compel that author to become a Muslim. We don't, they're not, and we haven't done.

With that much in the way of proem, we may begin.

The threats to speech and publication

I n late July, shortly before he ended up in hospital, Mr Pyle was confronting enemies of free speech: secular, political enemies, who wished to denigrate and silence their opponents, guillotine debate, and —under the usual rubric of 'hate speech' (which, naturally, *they* should define for the rest of us) —*litigate* (with a view to prohibiting) both the publication and the review of published papers in the social sciences. Their stance was clear and unashamed: dissent and debate must be cut off, and no one save themselves had the right to speak on the topics they designated.[5]

The situation has not improved —indeed it has markedly deteriorated — in the weeks since.

Yet this is not a new phenomenon. After a period in which, thankfully, we in the West had achieved consensus upon these undoubted, inherent human rights, to speak and to publish, being liable only for slander, libel, and the direct and immediate incitement to violent disorder in terms that should lead *reasonable hearers or readers immediately to resort to violent disorder,* there has been a retrograde movement: much of it the doing of the Left, cloaking their purpose in appeals to civility, appeals to happy-clappy 'unity', and the bogey of their rickety construct, 'hate speech' (boo, hiss! It

---

[5] Yes, of *course* there shall a Position Paper on the underlying topic in due course.

sounds villainous —and is calculated to do).

In fact, the Left have attempted to erect a 'right' —gleefully seized upon by the Radical Right on the Continent and by Islamists everywhere —'not to be offended'.

No such right exists.

To claim a right is to claim its universality, its universal application. Of course there are occasions upon which two actual rights conflict: the few exceptions to the rights of free speech and publication are founded in the obvious and acknowledged rights of privacy, of freedom from being libelled or slandered, and of being kept safe from the attacks of an incited mob.[6] But a 'right not to be offended' is simply ludicrous in principle. If anyone may claim it, then all may claim it, and assert it without being required to show any good faith or any reasoned justification for it: which leads immediately to a complete abandonment of the undoubted rights of free speech and publication, for which men have fought and died and rebelled, been gaoled and emerged to topple governments. If, on the other hand, it is a right that can be asserted only upon a *prior* showing[7] to a magistrate that the person asserting the right has some *special* reason for doing so, it is not a right. If the magistrate grants it, it is instead a privilege. And if it is dependent upon the State to grant or deny, *as* a privilege, it is the death of free speech and it inserts the State into deciding which individuals and which groups do or do not have a right to be offended *and to be legally protected against having their precious feelings hurt*, as distinct from the citizenry or subjects as a

---

[6] And that incitement must be immediate, clear, intended, *and calculated irresistibly to incite reasonable people.*
[7] Note the distinction – in terms of prohibiting publication and exercising a prior restraint upon speech – between this and bringing an action at law for damages, or indeed for injunctive relief, upon a claim of libel.

whole.

And of course that is precisely its intent: to become a privilege reserved to certain identity groups: gays,[8] lesbians, Leftists, Islamists, racial minorities, or what have you. It is simply censorship in favour of Approved Groups, in a new guise ('MILTON![9] Thou shouldst be living at this hour': no one's bloody read the *Areopagitica,* evidently).

Look it the claimed 'right' as applied. Imagine were we to gather a number of signatories on a petition against the now common habit, in the UK, of serving, without labelling or warning, halal food to all patrons: some signatories asserting that, as evangelical Christians, they are offended by this in light of the vision of St Peter regarding the dispensation from dietary rules (the Acts of the Apostles, the tenth chapter, beginning at the ninth verse: here endeth the Lesson), others asserting offence as animal-rights activists, yet others asserting themselves offended by it as Sikhs, to whom food slaughtered in this manner is forbidden. A panicked Cabinet should take to Cabinet Office Briefing Room (A) over it, and the House spend days on it. Better yet, imagine the inevitable clash between LGBT[10] activists and Islamists over the publication or performance of, well, damned near anything that touches upon gay issues: actually, you needn't in fact imagine it, because it's happening and has been happening for some time.

This alleged 'right' is nothing more —and nothing less —than the erection, or the attempted erection, of a new scheme of censorship, and one

---

[8] Mr Wemyss hastens to say that he'd not have such a 'right' or privilege as a bloody gift, ta ever sodding so. He can think of any number of fellow gayers who are of the same opinion as he.

[9] John, the poet, although Milton Friedman should do as well. Indeed, Milton Berle should do as well in the fight against the censor.

[10] Add whatever further initials you like to the increasingly unwieldy initialism. Mr Wemyss' view is that it already sounds like a lettuce, guacamole, bacon, and tomato sandwich in an American delicatessen.

not of universal application, but, rather, to be exercised in favour of State-favoured groups. Worse yet, it is the erection, or the attempted erection, of a heckler's *and a terrorist's* veto over free speech.

And its advocates quite often know this, guiltily. Observe the hypocrisy. The *New York Times* on 2 October 1999, editorialising on the exhibition 'Sensation' at the Brooklyn Museum of Art,[11] which featured Serrano's crucifix-in-a-jar-of-piss and Ofili's portrait of the BVM with naked arses and elephant shit,[12] set out for the unwashed its 'ground rules for government financing of cultural institutions *and the political censorship of constitutionally guaranteed freedom of expression*', saying, 'many citizens of conscience find parts of the Brooklyn exhibition repugnant, and it is understandable that many Roman Catholics would find Chris Ofili's image of the Virgin Mary offensive.[13] Others would agree with our colleague William Safire that while the Brooklyn Museum has a right to show what it likes, the administrators have been clumsy or needlessly provocative. Yet [...] [a] museum is obliged to challenge the public as well as to placate it, or else the museum becomes a chamber of attractive ghosts, an institution completely disconnected from art in our time. [...] We are confident the court will see the city's arguments for what they are —a pretext to justify the Mayor's anger at a museum that dared to defend artistic freedom.'

On 12 September 2012, however, weighing in on the Salafist mob's violence —violence alleged (quite incredibly: the assertion is self-evidently

---

[11] *Can* one write or read that without cognitive dissonance? It's as if the Tate were in Swindon.

[12] People have become blasé about this old controversy. We use these terms advisedly to remind people just how outraged many were at the time: sufficiently so that the *New York Times* felt it necessary to admonish the 'oiks' from its plane of self-assumed Moral Superiority. (If these ghastly little people at that puerile fish-wrap are an elite, America's buggered.)

[13] Evidently, the hacks didn't know any Eastern or Greek Orthodox or any Anglican High Churchmen.

rubbish) to have been a spontaneous reaction to a clip of a film which, unlike the 'Sensations' exhibition and the rubbishing 'art' in it, was *not* publicly funded by the long-suffering US ratepayer —the *New York Times* had something very different to say: that '[h]owever offensive the video is, it could never justify the violence in Benghazi and Cairo. But —' ah, the inevitable 'but' —'Mr. Jones, Mr. Sadek and whoever made the film did true damage to the interests of the United States and its core principle of respecting all faiths.'[14]

This is rank hypocrisy: positively noisome. What motivates it? The obvious answer is, of course, simple cravenness. Cowardice, full stop, *tout court.* The squeaking wheel gets the grease, the dog in the manger wins out, and the mad dog heckler-cum-terrorist prevails.

Consider the playwright Terrence McNally and his play, *Corpus Christi.*[15] There were, shamefully, 'cultural' and 'social' 'conservatives' who objected to it, and to its being performed.[16] There were, it is alleged, death threats; and it was hastily and conveniently presumed that these were from outraged Christians.[17] But, as the Beeb reported on 29 October 1999, when the play opened in London —and it did open, as it had opened in Australia despite episcopal anathemata, and as it had opened in America, and as it had opened in Edinburgh for all the dour complaints —what Mr McNally was

---

[14] It must be said at once that there is no such 'core principle' in the United States. Just you try and find it in the Constitution, or imagine making such a claim to Hamilton, Madison, Jay, Monroe, Franklin, and Washington, or to Patrick Henry, George Wythe, and the Anti-Federalists. You'd have been lucky to escape with your hide, and thanked your God that Jefferson was in Paris and unable to get at you.

[15] Not the Feast; not the College, or the Tab one at that Other Place in the Fens; and not the Texas coastal town. The play depicts Christ and the Apostles as young gay men living on the Texas Gulf Coast: slash-fiction, *Bible* fandom.

[16] These are the people who decry censorship in favour of Islamists whilst demanding that flag-burning be criminalised. Sigh.

[17] And may have been: the point being that the press failed of its duty to find out and report, *because it is politicised to the point of intellectual dishonesty.*

faced with was a *fatwa* (for Muslims consider Jesus to have been a prophet second only, on their view, to Muhammad) from the *soi-disant* 'Shari'ah Court of the UK' and its 'sheikh', one Omar Bakri Muhammad (né Fostock, of all unlikely surnames). (Yes, the terror-supporting bugger and long-time benefits claimant, who celebrated 11 September and 7 July: the midwife of Hizb ut-Tahrir in the United Kingdom, head of Al-Muhajiroun, and purveyor of messages from UBL: a busy life for a man on the dole. *That* sod.) In addition to ... *explosive* ... theatre criticism, of course, Mr Bakri is noted for music criticism ('If he values his life, [Sir Paul] McCartney must not come to Israel. He will not be safe there. The sacrifice operatives will be waiting for him') and literary criticism ('[Sir Salman] Rushdie will continue living his life in hiding. Any *fatwa* will stand until it is fulfilled. He is always going to be worried about a Muslim reaching him').

Now, Mr Bakri is not precisely taken seriously; but from the initial *fatwa* over *The Satanic Verses* forwards, and certainly from the London première of Mr McNally's little play unto this day,[18] the Left has been tying itself increasingly in knots trying to square their *bien-pensant,* muesli-munching, sandalled, *Grauniadista* pieties with their inexplicable support of the poor, downtrodden Muslims —and the sheer terror they feel, with loosened bowels and quaking knees, at crossing Salafists whose response to free speech, let alone to being gay-friendly, consists in bombs and beheadings.

But of course this sort of thing isn't always the fruit of sheer, teeth-chattering, pants-wetting funk. Sometimes it is the fruit of ineffable stupidity; and occasionally, of simple disloyalty to the ideal of these rights of

---

[18] Having mentioned Mr McNally's puerility, a palate-cleanser from Willy the Shake is always in order.

free speech and freedom of publication: adherence, that is to say, to their enemies. The result is in any case the same: what Orwell called, quite rightly, objective fascism.

The common thread

Let us take a closer look at recent threats to free speech and freedom of publication, and see what they have in common — and what those who advocate against free speech and freedom of publication have in common.

In 2010, a man named Andrew Stack deliberately flew his light aeroplane into an Internal Revenue field office in Austin, Texas. Although he left behind a suicide manifesto quoting Marx, railing against George W Bush, and attributing part of his fury against government to the lack of socialised medicine in the US —a screed that was approved with only *pro forma* reservations by Noam Chomsky in a 20 April 2010 article, 'Remembering Fascism: Learning From the Past', carried at truthout.org —the Left and the press (but we repeat ourselves) rushed to characterise the act as that of a Rabid Tea-Partier.™ When Congresswoman Gabrielle Giffords was shot in an attempted assassination by a gibbering gibbon named Jared Loughner — who, insofar as he was not an apolitical nutter, was a Lefty stoner —it was immediately alleged that he had been inspired and incited by the Tea Party and Sarah Palin. In both cases, the corollary was that those *not* on the Left, who were by that very fact somehow guilty by association, must cease to speak, to 'watch their tone',[19] to moderate their statements, and to censor

---

[19] It is amusing, in a morbid sort of way, to realise that the online Left is forever searching feverishly for anything that can be represented as constituting an admonition by non-Leftists to 'mind *their* tone', which is, to them, a punishable blasphemy and a clear evidence of Oppression and Repression (in the Dennis the Peasant sense: 'Come and see the violence inherent in the system. 'Elp! 'Elp! I'm being repressed!').

themselves.

The centre and the Right are not blameless either. It is well within anyone's rights to boycott or support one or another play, or book, or indeed fast-food chicken restaurant, and to condemn any author, any work, any publisher: *as an exercise of free speech.* Corporations and private institutions may decline to give space, support, a hearing, and lashings of dosh to anyone they damned well please, if they are displeased by someone or his views or his work. But *as an exercise of a universal freedom,* these criticisms and condemnations end, full stop, at a red line, before reaching the point at which they attempt to use the law and the State, or threats against public order and safety, to prohibit the *exercise of a universal freedom by others* to read, write, publish, paint, act in, or watch anything they damned well please (so long as it's not snuff films[20] or kiddie-fiddling or that sort of thing, obviously). What the centre-right (which is all save the most palæolithic of palæo-conservatives in America: American 'conservatives', bar the so-called 'cultural "conservatives"' and the most primitive Palæo-Cons of the Buchananite-Paulite fever swamps, are classical Liberals) must realise, is a quite simple point. No one could call Gerald Ford a 'movement Conservative'; but he told the Republican Party something that Lady Thatcher could as easily have said.[21] He reminded them, 'A government big enough to give you everything you want is a government big enough to take from you everything you have.'

That is true not only of the political and economic threat of government intervention. It is equally true, or more so, of the threat to morals. If you *will* persist in endowing the State and the government of the day with the

---

[20] This has nothing to do with one's tobacconist.
[21] If not as regarded Section 28, then certainly as regarded Sunday opening.

power and authority, the appearance of legitimacy, to impose your moral standards upon your fellow subjects, you have granted the next government cover to do the same. And sooner or later, that government are going to contain a majority which is utterly and wholly of a different view of morality to yours.

But let us go on. It is in the culture, more even than in the political, wars, that we see these threats asserted most frequently. Take poor old Salman Rushdie. His publication of *The Satanic Verses* was, in its unintended consequences, a major turning-point in the fight for these freedoms. He has lived ever since under a *fatwa*. His translators abroad have been subject to assassination attempts, a brace of which have succeeded. Protests and threats —even against HM the Queen, after he got a K to go with his *fatwa*[22] – have never really ceased; there are bounties on his head; he was quite likely the intended victim, as his knighthood was the pretext, for a failed bombing attempt in London; bookshops were bombed; and the failed (and really quite idiotic) private prosecution brought against him by Muslim barristers[23] for blasphemous libel resulted, at long last, in the elimination of blasphemy laws from the statute book.

If, however, when *The Satanic Verses* were published and again when Rushdie got his K, there were those who covered themselves in glory in standing up for free speech and the freedom to publish, there were others who, to use a guid Scots term in place of what we're really thinking, covered themselves in glaur. Some Muslim leaders on the Continent dissented from the *fatwa*, bless them, and were killed (damn the buggers who did it). The

---

[22] Bloody cheek. Indeed, damned impertinence. You do *not* threaten HMQ.
[23] Quite inexcusably. Disgrace to their Inns, that lot.

bungle-wallahs[24] of Islamic politics in the UK beclowned themselves; the (Usually-Sounder-Than-This) then Chief Rabbi, afterward Lord Jakobovits, and the then Archbishop of Canterbury, that reliably useless invertebrate Runcie, supported extending the blasphemy laws to cover Islam and prohibit books like Rushdie's; Roald Dahl embarrassed himself mightily; and —of course —Jimmy Carter made a classic 'of course I believe in free speech *but*' apologia. John Berger and John Le Carré betrayed any principles they might have been thought to have had by calling upon Rushdie to withdraw the book.

And it yet goes on. Literary festivals in India dissolve into macabre farce over the book even now; and Ayatollah Hassan Sanei,[25] the right-hand (or perhaps more appropriately the left-hand)[26] man of the late Ayatollah Khomeini, who issued the Rushdie *fatwa,* has seized upon the latest round of Islamist riots and murders to up the bounty on Rushdie, saying, of the film that is the current pretext for infantile rage, that it 'won't be the last insulting act as long as Imam Khomeini's historic order on executing the blasphemous Salman Rushdie is not carried out. If the imam's order was [poor bugger means, 'had been'] carried out, the further insults in the form of caricatures, articles, and films would not have taken place. The impertinence of the grudge-filled enemies of Islam, which is occurring under the flag of the Great Satan, America, and the racist Zionists, can only be blocked [or, actually, 'be blocked only'; who translates this balls, and does he, actually, speak English?] by the absolute administration of this Islamic order.'

---

[24] Whinge all you like, Inayat. You think we don't get stick for *our* surnames in a good polemical free-for-all?

[25] Please, *please,* tell us his middle initial is 'N'.

[26] Well, after all, he *is* a complete shit.

Let's look back a moment, shall we, to the inglorious responses of some people to Rushdie's inclusion in the Honours List in 2007. Labour's ghastly Lord Ahmed decried it —on the grounds (wait for it) of prudence and the giving of offence: 'this man has been very divisive. This man —as you can see —not only provoked violence around the world because of his writings, but there were many people that were killed around the world and honouring the man who has blood on his hands, sort of because of what he did, honouring him I think is going a bit too far'; disgracefully, the Conservative (at least nominally so) MP Stewart Jackson, the hon. Member for Peterborough and, significantly, the then Chairman of the All Party Parliamentary Group on Pakistan, complained that '[w]e do not need a situation where we are gratuitously offending our allies in the fight against terror'. (At the time, UBL was most likely in Pakistan: he was after all eventually found there, and killed, in Abbottabad, which is rather like finding, in 1955 or so, that an escaped Hitler had taken a cottage near Sandhurst ten years earlier and lived there rather freely since. Abbottabad is not precisely removed from the ken of the Pakistani State, or its State Within the State, the ISI. If Stewart Jackson regarded Pakistan at any time as an 'ally in the fight against terror', one almost sympathises with the yob who kicked the silly bugger at a bus shelter in his constituency.) Jack Straw waffled a bit before getting to the point: on the one hand —as if it mattered a damn —he expressed an appreciation of the 'concerns and sensitivity' in the Muslim community, before —on the other hand —quite properly insisting there was 'no justification whatever for suggestions that as a result of this a further *fatwa* should be placed on the life of Mr Rushdie' —as indeed there isn't. It was the rather unlikely triumvirate (if Ms Jowell doesn't mind being a *vir* for a moment)[27] of David Davis MP (the Dave we *ought* to have as PM, who was at the time the Shadow Home Secretary), the then Home Secretary John Reid, and the then Culture Secretary Tessa Jowell, who shone brightest, even as the MCB (hullo again, Inayat!) called the K a 'deliberate provocation' and rioters led by such gentry as Anjem Choudray screamed 'Death to Rushdie! Death to the Queen!'[28]

Mr Davis said that freedom of speech is a fundamental freedom, and that in any case, HM's acts as the fount of honour shall never be the subject of intimidation.[29] Dr Reid made the fundamental point that honours for services to letters are not predicated upon how many people agree with a writer's views, and that that was and should remain The British Way. And Ms Jowell pointed out that it was necessary then more than ever to stand for freedom of speech.

You, naturally, have already noted that the conflict here is one of people on one side taking offence and complaining —often murderously —of hurt feelings, and, upon the other side, people standing up for a universal right.

It remains so. The difference today is in who is on the right side of that quarrel.

Look here, damn it all, we're Anglicans. Insult our beliefs and we'll debate you if you like; if ever we were to wish to crack down on dissent sans debate, we'd offer you a choice of cake or death. (For some reason, everyone opts for cake.) The Holy Office nowadays —under Cardinals Ximenez and Fang, now that Cardinal Biggles has been translated to Pope —treats heresy very severely: with the comfy chair. Yet we seem to be outnumbered. Sir

---

[27] An old gag by a member of the Algonquin Round Table, if Mr Pyle recalls aright.

[28] And that, children, is where free speech *does* cross a line. Also, it's damned impertinence.

[29] Britons never, never, never shall be slaves. Rule, Britannia.

Salman was brought up a Muslim —he's not one now —and was and remains a Lefty luvvie. He may have expected that Muslims should Have Their Feelings Hurt by his book (and are sulking yet, if by sulking one means 'in many cases getting on with trying to kill him'); it must have been a shock, though, to find other Lefties, then and yet more nowadays, kicking him out of Lefty fandom.[30]

Why is this?

Let's keep going: we may just find out.

The assertion of this idiotic 'right not to be offended' as a means of compromising or throttling the actual rights to free speech and to freedom of publication occurs in a goodish number of contexts that seem superficially rather different. Oh, certainly there are the riots over Rushdie's book, cartoons in Norway, alleged incidents of Not Handling the Koran With the Respect its followers should like to see,[31] and All That. But it doesn't end there.

A friend of Mr Pyle's, in July, who is a supporter of extending the right to marry to same-sex couples, was aggrieved by an article that led her to condemn —indeed, the article incited the condemnation of —the American pundit and opponent of same-sex marriage, Maggie Gallagher. Mr Pyle's friend asserted that it was time to cease debating Ms Gallagher, based upon assertions that she was an evil person morally responsible for evil actions alleged and attributable to others.

Mr Pyle demurred. 'Hate to say it, but I have to disagree with you

---

[30] This is because they don't read canon, but, rather, (wait for it) Fanon.

[31] They seem to have an idea that it is - to borrow from St John - the Word incarnated (although of course it's not, strictly speaking, an incarnation); that the Real Presence of God is in each copy of the book. This seems rather close to material idolatry to us, but the whole point of freedom is the right to let them think what they like, let us think it very queer indeed, *and to not cut up rough when we bloody well say as much.*

here.... Judging folks by their faces is several sorts of informal fallacy; I've never seen any evidence that Ms Gallagher wants anyone to hurry up and die, and I cannot imagine any valid argument that changing or not changing a legal doctrine about the *ius matrimonium* has anything to do with such an assertion (which would in any case be an *argumentum ad consequentiam*); there's a valid point to be made that —so far as the argument is clear — proponents of rewriting millennia of common law are engaged in *petitio:* to assert that (1) an argument (2) over whether or not something is and must be recognized as a "civil right," (3) is foreclosed by (4) *presuming* and *asserting* that it *is* [such a right], sans debate, is an obvious flaw in reasoning; and I'll be damned if I can *ever* agree with the proposition that something mustn't be debated, any more than I'll agree to the SPLC's assertions making an appeal to authority *contra,* valid.'[32]

Into this friendly and reasoned debate between two reasonable friends there entered a person named Scott Rose, who, it appears, is —in one of our better modern oxymorons —an 'advocacy journalist' with Strong Views. Mr Rose, in tones and with reasoning that any radical imam should envy, made the following post, a public one, here reprinted without correction or elision:

> Markham Shaw Pyle FUCK YOU! FUCK YOU! FUCK YOU
> FOR WRITING THAT YOU HAVEN"T SEEN ANY
> EVIDENCE THAT MAGGOT GAGGIN-WHORE[33] THINKS

---

[32] Mr Pyle's objection to the fallacy of appeal to authority *contra* is universal. His specific objection to the resort to the Southern Poverty Law Centre *as* that authority derives from his distrust of a law firm, shilling for business, that has labelled perfectly reputable historians of the XIXth Century as 'neo-Confederate' hate-mongers. The SPLC did a good work in running Kluxers out of public life; but having done so, it chose not to disband, but, rather, to gin up new threats and new clients by having non-scholars create groups of hate figures whom it could then accuse of being purveyors of hate.

[33] This is Mr Rose's charming term for Ms Maggie Gallagher. Note that his belief in the Righteousness of the Elect - in whom he makes one - excuses to his mind what he decries in others.

THAT THE ONLY GOOD GAY IS A DEAD GAY. Even if the topic were not the death of gays, Gagginwhore has written that she is "unwilling" to live in a country that gives anti-discrimination protections to homosexuals — that includes in hiring and in lodgings. Maggot Gagginwhore's organization sponsors anti-gay hate rallies where its speakers yell through megaphones that homosexuals are "worthy to death." NOM's head Robert George also is on the board of the SPLC-certified anti-gay hate group, the Family Research Council. And btw, YOUR FUCKING SACK OF UNEDUCATED SHIT —the main reason that the SPLC classifies a group as an anti-gay hate group, is that the group repeatedly promulgates known falsehoods against gay people. Such as, fraudulently conflating homosexuals with pedophiles, and encouraging the public to believe that all homosexuals are pedophiles. That why the FRC[34] is a hate group —among other KNOWN FALSEHOODS that it continually spreads against gay people, with the intent to keep them living as second-class citizens. Robert George mentored evangelicals who went to Uganda and hate-mongered against homosexuals, so strongly that the government there proposed the infamous "Kill the gays!" law. Ugandan tabloids started publishing the names and addresses of known homosexuals and calling for their executions; many such executions were actually carried out. CA Congressman Brad Sherman proposed a congressional resolution against Uganda's violations of its gay citizens' human rights, and Robert George's FRC spent $35K lobbying AGAINST the resolution, on grounds it constituted "pro-homosexual promotion." And Maggot Gagginwhore says that she "cherishes" working with the FRC. Get it, fuckface? The group says you can't condemn a country's leadership for permitting gangland style executions of known gay people, because to do so would constitute pro-homosexual promotion. Oh and one other thing, asshole; you reference to "rewriting millennia of common law;" firstly, that's white ethnocentric. Most Native American tribes honored same sex long term relationships, including those in which the same sex couples raised children. OUR RIGHTS ARE NOT FOR AN ASSHOLE LIKE YOU TO DEBATE.

---

[34] The NOM is the National Organisation for Marriage. The FRC is the Family Research Council.

Right. Let's think about that for a moment, shall we. Not the merits of the underlying dispute, which are a subject for another Paper;[35] not the mere vulgar abuse; nor yet the fallacies and bad reasoning: rather, let's consider that final shriek. 'Our rights are not for an asshole like you to debate.'[36]

A century ago, Chesterton noted the rise of "the New Bigotry":

> I notice with some amusement, both in America and English literature, the rise of a new kind of bigotry. Bigotry does not consist in a man being convinced he is right; that is not bigotry, but sanity. Bigotry consists in a man being convinced that another man must be wrong in everything, because he is wrong in a particular belief; that he must be wrong, even in thinking that he honestly believes he is right.

This seems to have been an occasion on which GKC's prescience was operating properly — and that despite his having notoriously and inexcusably been wrong in one particular and highly significant belief, not implicated in the above.

Mr Rose, based upon his published screeds on the internet, all of them, so far as one can see, concerning this issue and gay rights generally, seems honestly to believe that those who do not agree with him are wicked people

---

[35] To get it out of the way in brief, now: our view is that the State has no business in the consensual sexual conduct of any two or more competent adults, freely contracting; that civil unions / civil partnerships are fine and dandy so long as democratically chosen and not imposed upon a political entity by judicial ukase; and that marriage is a bundle of special rights and special responsibilities, implicating everything from agency and fiduciary law to intestate succession to, in many jurisdictions, the rules of evidence; and the only possible justification for the State's granting these special privileges to, and imposing these special burdens on, any two people, is not that they happen to be in love, but that they are a man and a woman *whom the law presumes shall have issue:* the purpose of marriage, legally, being to create an estate out of the in-laws' heritable property to be managed by spouses so as to descend to the issue of the marriage. Marriage is a device for the orderly descent and distribution of heritable property, and that is its sole purpose and sole justification *in the eyes of the civil, secular law.*

[36] Mr Rose wrote this not many days prior to the Chik-Fil-A boycott and counter-boycott, and the political shootings at the FRC offices in Washington. *By the standards now being applied by the Left to That Video,* he 'incited' the shootings and is an 'accessory'. Of course, he isn't: *any more than is – or should be were the riots in fact due to That Video – Mr Nakoula as regards the current riots.*

who must be destroyed, very nearly by any means necessary. He has attempted to bring, and may by now *have* brought, an action at law against a university, a scholar, and a peer-reviewed publication in the social sciences, all because he disagrees with a paper and has convinced himself that it is an evil deed, corruptly funded and published through some wicked conspiracy. He has sought to have his political opponents prosecuted. And he appears to be completely convinced that those who disagree with him *ought not to have the freedom to debate him.* It is difficult to characterise this as anything save the return of the paranoid style in American politics, to its natural home on the Left; indeed, it is very difficult not to see it as a classic sample of McCarthyism. 'Our rights are not for an asshole like you to debate.' It really does suggest that Tailgunner Joe is alive, well, and working for the Left.

There is really only one thing which one can say to this —it having been said best, long ago, by Mill:

> Let us suppose, therefore, that the government is entirely at one with the people, and never thinks of exerting any power of coercion unless in agreement with what it conceives to be their voice. But I deny the right of the people to exercise such coercion, either by themselves or by their government. The power itself is illegitimate. The best government has no more title to it than the worst. It is as noxious, or more noxious, when exerted in accordance with public opinion, than when in opposition to it. If all mankind minus one, were of one opinion, and only one person were of the contrary opinion, mankind would be no more justified in silencing that one person, than he, if he had the power, would be justified in silencing mankind. Were an opinion a personal possession of no value except to the owner; if to be obstructed in the enjoyment of it were simply a private injury, it would make some difference whether the injury was inflicted only on a few persons or on many. *But the peculiar evil of silencing the expression*

of an opinion is, that it is robbing the human race; posterity as well as the existing generation; those who dissent from the opinion, still more than those who hold it. If the opinion is right, they are deprived of the opportunity of exchanging error for truth: if wrong, they lose, what is almost as great a benefit, the clearer perception and livelier impression of truth, produced by its collision with error.

It is necessary to consider separately these two hypotheses, each of which has a distinct branch of the argument corresponding to it. *We can never be sure that the opinion we are endeavouring to stifle is a false opinion; and if we were sure, stifling it would be an evil still.*

We'll come back to that in a moment.

Let's examine another Leftist —we're really terribly sorry, but it *is* the Left who are making the running with this —who wishes to forbid debate by his opponents. His name is Brett Kimberlin. Today, he is a Leftist activist who runs the non-profits Justice Through Music Project and Velvet Revolution, funded by the Usual Suspects. More to the point, he is a convicted domestic terrorist —the 'Speedway Bomber' —and perjurer, having started out as a trafficker in drugs.[37] Bloggers —Left, Right, and Centre —who have had the temerity to report these facts (and, in light of these facts, to question, not unnaturally, the expenditures and management of these non-profits) have, at the least, been subjected to 'lawfare': an endless string of, quite frankly, frivolous lawsuits filed by Mr Kimberlin.

---

[37] See, *e.g., United States v. Kimberlin,* 805 F.2d 210 (7th Cir.1986), cert. denied, 483 U.S. 1023, 107 S.Ct. 3270, 97 L.Ed.2d 768 (1987); *United States v. Kimberlin,* 781 F.2d 1247 (7th Cir.1985), cert. denied, 479 U.S. 938, 107 S.Ct. 419, 93 L.Ed.2d 370 (1986); *United States v. Kimberlin,* 692 F.2d 760 (7th Cir.1982) (table), cert. denied, 460 U.S. 1092, 103 S.Ct. 1792, 76 L.Ed.2d 359 (1983); *United States v. Kimberlin,* 673 F.2d 1335 (7th Cir.1981) (table), cert. denied, 456 U.S. 964, 102 S.Ct. 2044, 72 L.Ed.2d 489 (1982); and on subsequent collateral attack, *United States v. Kimberlin,* 898 F.2d 1262 (7th Cir.), cert. denied, 498 U.S. 969, 111 S.Ct. 434, 112 L.Ed.2d 417 (1990). See further, *United States v. Kimberlin,* 776 F.2d 1344 (7th Cir.1985), cert. denied, 476 U.S. 1142, 106 S.Ct. 2251, 90 L.Ed.2d 697 (1986); *United States v. Kimberlin,* 675 F.2d 866 (7th Cir.1982). It takes effort to commit perjury to a Federal grand jury before you graduate high school. Mr Kimberlin managed.

(Odder things yet have befallen his opponents, but there is not —*yet* —proof that he is behind them.) Now that Mr Kimberlin has been sued in his turn, after one of his frivolous actions went very badly for him, he is resisting discovery as of the time of writing.

If this reminds you rather of one Julian Assange ... you're not wrong. They don't like it up them.

(To get the usual Leaky Wick whingery out of the way: one of the few exceptions we are willing to admit to the right of free speech and freedom of publication is the protection of *legitimate* diplomatic and military secrets. Mr Assange and his needy, seedy crew[38] apparently believe, or profess to believe, that free speech entails, say, embedding Lord Haw-Haw with the troops going ashore in Normandy, and allowing him to broadcast the order of battle, dispositions, plans, and troop numbers to Berlin. This is puerile. Woodrow Wilson was — as not infrequently he was — wrong about diplomatic secrecy. On the other hand, we, unlike a certain religion professor at Penn, to whom we shall shortly turn, do not believe that freedom to publish and freedom of speech should contemplate prior restraint —unless one is a war correspondent in the midst of battle —by the military.)

And so we come to the video clip, *The Innocence of Muslims,* and its purported role in provoking riot and murder in North Africa, the Levant, and by now just about everywhere with a considerable Muslim population bar Bradford.

Let us be frank. It almost certainly played no role in these mob scenes —

---

[38] The reference, appositely, is to such 'objective fascists', including Stalinists during the period of the Molotov-Ribbentrop Pact, as Sir Oswald Mosley, Harry Pollitt, and Archibald Maule Ramsay MP. It is taken from the earl Winterton's remarks to the House on 7 May 1940.

it was no coincidence that they occurred, after much evident planning, on 11 September —*and it shouldn't matter a damn if it did*. Nor shall we pause for the ritual denunciation of its merits: those also are absolutely immaterial. The right of free expression is as near to absolute as damn it. And incitement is actionable only if it was reasonably calculated immediately to overwhelm and thus incite *reasonable* people.

Persons believing themselves to have a right not to be offended, and a right to attack any who offend them, are — *eo ipso* – absolutely *not* reasonable.

Quite bluntly, there is no right not to be offended; and, what is more, If your conception of an omnipotent Deity requires that his mortal creatures defend his honour and vindicate his dignity by force of arms, your conception is self-evidently ludicrous. If your religion has its own Brezhnev Doctrine, it's self-evidently false. And if these statements enrage you ... that is precisely *your* problem.

We are absolutely serious when we say that neither artistic merit, nor good manners, is or may permissibly be made the measure of whether speech may be allowed and be protected. In fact, with the very few exceptions we have outlined, it is our view that speech and expression, and consequently publication, performance, or exhibition, is *presumptively* free and protected, with the onus upon its opponents to demonstrate conclusively why *and on what agreed ground of exception* it ought to be limited. That is not only our view: it is the natural right of mankind, for which revolutions have been carried through, wars fought, and martyrs made. (Note that no one has ever set the world afire *and raised the hearts of free men and women with his struggle and his clarion cry* for the sake of being free from having his widdle feelings hurt.)

Recall this: not only is there and must there be an all but absolute right to speak and to publish; there is and must be an all but absolute right to *be spoken to,* to hear. You mayn't like what someone has to say, but you have *no* right to prevent his saying it *so that* we *may hear it:* particularly if it is something we'd rather not hear.

Contemplate for a moment a world in which the right to express oneself were predicated upon artistic merit in the expression. There'd be some 1K of traffic a day on the Net. Newspapers should be printed on postcards. Books should be burnt for fuel. And of course the question should be, Who determines artistic merit? *For those persons should then become the unaccountable dictators of the world.* (Imagine were it we —which is far likelier than its being the Left, with all their proudly 'transgressive' minority tastes —and that we were corrupted by that absolute power rather than remaining the Thoroughly Nice Chaps we are. Vermeer, Cuyp, Hobbema, and Potter should be regarded with almost religious awe. Ownership of a Stubbs, a Munning, or a Frith —or in America, a Remington or a Russell — should grant one a peerage. Picassos should be put in a cellar to moulder; and Serrano and Ofili should be banged up in HMP Pentonville, not for blasphemy, but for the Cockney impudence of charging the public, in guineas, for flinging a jar of pee and a chamberpot in the public's face. It's damned nearly fraud to call that 'art' —but it's protected expression all the same.)

Or imagine a world in which mannerly speech alone were acceptable speech, and all speech remained even so subject to prosecution by anyone who chose to take offence. One can see it now:

'One moment. Constable, what reason did Mr Paulet give for giving Mr Seymour in charge?'

''E said, my Lord, as the prisoner 'ad wished him "Good morning"; and he said, my Lord, that 'e —Mr Paulet, I mean —'ad a bugger of an 'angover, and in any case 'e was goin' to 'ave the sort o' mornin' 'e damned well pleased, my Lord, and that it was an Englishman's right to 'ave any sort of mornin' 'e chose, and if this sort o' thing was to be allowed, my Lord, the next thing'd be people demanding that one 'ave a nice day, like a lot of bloody Yanks.'

'And a very sound statement of the law it was, too. I shall direct the jury accordingly. Go on, Constable.'

Quite seriously, it seems to us madness that a Left who identify themselves so strongly with political and religious (or anti-religious) views not held by, and indeed loathed by, the majority of their fellow subjects and fellow citizens, and who are allowed to hold and express those views in Western democracies only by virtue of these protected rights, should be so prone to urging that these rights be limited, repressed, or disallowed. Presumably they believe that they are the Elect and shall then have a monopoly on free exercise of these freedoms, and the power to deny these freedoms to others; but surely they cannot be quite *that* bloody thick? A rather backwards adolescent baboon —and we have always considered that the Left are at least (and commonly at most) *that* clever —could readily see that the power to reclaim those freedoms from their intrusion, were they somehow to seize the machinery of the State, either in government or in the Civil Service, and launch an *open* attack upon the rights they have been attempting to subvert covertly for some years, rests in the majority. And those who would set the constitution at naught want to recall that the Forces are sworn to its ultimate defence. Were a gaggle of redbrick dons (or their American equivalents in whatever SCRs the Yanks have) to attempt to suppress these freedoms in a way that was obvious, they or their puppets in office should be swept aside, by ballots; and should they then decline to abide that arbitrament, well: the average squaddie, and the average US soldier, worship very different gods than do the Left.

Yet look at the reactions to the latest global Islamist tantrum. These are people, alas, who, when they throw their dummies out of the pram, kill bystanders with them. We don't accept that all or even a major part of this ongoing tanty was occasioned by a cheap film clip on the Net; but some of those throwing the fit assert that, and all of those whose reactions we now survey believe, or pretend to believe, that that clip was the cause of this murderously puerile reaction.

Very well: in that case, it is a straight fight between free speech and its enemies, the latter being gathered at this juncture beneath the banner of Having a Right Not to Be Offended By Anything Ever.

It is blazingly obvious which is the right side in *that* dispute: that of free speech. The regimental colours for *our* side bear battle honours that take one's breath away, and the mess portraits include such past officers and notable Other Ranks as Locke, Milton, Orwell, Coke, Blackstone, Shelley, and Blake.

But who are these arrayed against free speech?

Well, there's the US State Department; the US Department of Justice; Secretary Clinton, Attorney-General Holder, the Pentagon, the Joint Chiefs, and President Obama. They have all acknowledged the professed right of Muslims —and so far, Muslims only —Not to Be Offended By Anything Ever. US diplomats have been murdered, and the US government are not only going on with the fiction that it was That Film that provoked the murders (incidentally contradicting, indeed giving the lie direct to, the Libyan government's statements), they are taking the position that That Film ought not to have been made *and running apologetic adverts on Pakistani television.*

It gives us no pleasure to defend Mr Nakoula, who seems a nasty piece of work —assuming for the moment that he is indeed 'Sam Bacile' —and who in that case might well be liable to be sued to his last farthing by the actors he hired *if* in fact he misled them about the film and exposed them to all this. Nor can one condone the initial and mischievous claims that 'Sam Bacile' was a Jew and an Israeli whose film was funded by Jewish investors. But these are civil matters; we are concerned with the criminalisation or governmental suppression of free speech and the freedom to publish. And in that context, *it is not only necessary, it is an absolute moral obligation,* to defend the rights of speech and speakers one holds and justly holds in contempt.[39]

If your commitment to free speech and freedom of publication is limited to defending instances of expression which you do not find contemptible, *you are not in fact in favour of free speech and freedom of publication.*

If your commitment to free speech and freedom of publication is

---

[39] Regrettably, Sir Salman Rushdie has made one of those who declines to defend even Mr Nakoula's rights, on the ground that he knew what he was getting into: the very criticism advanced against Rushdie then and again the other day in the *Guardian* by those who declined to defend *him*. Defending free speech truly *does* require that one defend some ghastly people ... Sir Salman.

limited to defending instances of expression which do not happen to offend you, *you are not in fact in favour of free speech and freedom of publication.*

If your commitment to free speech and freedom of publication is limited to defending instances of expression which do not happen to offend others, *you are not in fact in favour of free speech and freedom of publication.*

Mr Pyle is not the only one of us who becomes entangled in free speech debates on the Net. For some days now, Mr Wemyss, with Mr David Harsanyi and Mr Sam Schulman, has been engaged in a conversation on Twitter with the gelded appeasers at the US Embassy in Cairo and with what appears to be a well-meaning young person, apparently Muslim and apparently American, in which colloquy Mr Wemyss, with unwonted patience, has attempted to explain these points gently. The well-meaning young person appears to be struggling with the concept, because he (presumably 'he') has fallen prey to the siren lure of 'hate speech' as a construct.

This is a construct that must be rejected *in toto.*[40] It is ~~the means whereby the camel gets its nose under the tent~~[41] the thin end of the wedge.

Who defines 'hate speech' —particularly when it is joined with the alleged Right Not to Be Offended By Anything Ever and Never to Have One's Ickle Feelings Hurted, Aww? Because whosoever has the right to define some expressions as being 'hate speech' and thus *to remove from such statements the protection of the law, in denial of the right of free speech and the freedom to publish,* has acquired tyrannical powers over the rest of us.

---

[40] I've got you now, my pretty, and your little dog, too. (Fear not: Dorothy has a friend in Mr Wemyss.)

[41] It might very well be argued to be a criminal offence nowadays to use that metaphor in England and Wales. Which rather proves our point.

Tyrannical power? Oh, assuredly. Look at how it is used. It is an absolute scandal that journalists sat on their hands — which weren't, therefore, tapping keys or holding pens —over the prosecution of Andrew Bolt. It is an absolute scandal that journalists sat on their hands when Ezra Levant and Mark Steyn were being dragged through various kangaroo courts — the Orwellianly-named 'Human Rights' commissions and tribunals that infest Canada.

Some journalists, and rather more *writers,* took a stand for freedom. But all too many others have done far worse than sit on their hands.

No one likes defending Mr Nakoula, but if his rights are subject to revocation, so are yours and ours and everyone else's. Yet what did the US administration of Mr Obama do? It condemned Mr Nakoula rather more fiercely than it did the mobs, mullahs, and murderers.[42] In fact, in a scene that was until now utterly unimaginable in America, Mr Nakoula was dragged from his home in the middle of the night and taken away in a classic American 'perp walk', a tactic designed to poison the public mind against him. Nor was it out of consideration for his safety or that of his neighbours that this was done at night: for it was done in the full glare of a three-ring media circus almost designed —perhaps indeed designed —to tell *fatwa-*crazed Islamists, 'Over here! This is his house! Bombs away!'. Nor is it anything but the most feeble of pretexts to pretend, as the administration pretends, that Mr Nakoula was 'voluntarily answering questions' and was asked to do so only because he has, as Mr Kimberlin has, a past conviction.[43]

---

[42] Curious, really, when one considers that the mobs, mullahs, and murderers are *par excellence* those who 'get bitter, they cling to guns or religion or antipathy to people who aren't like them'....

[43] We of all people are not disbelievers in redemption. Anyone may be led astray when young or when desperate or when *bouleversé.* Even dear Mr Fry erred in his youth. Nevertheless, it is legitimate to remark the fact – something Mr Kimberlin refuses to countenance or to understand.

He is clearly 'assisting the police with their enquiries' in the British sense of that term.[44] This was a nakedly obvious capitulation to the enemies of free speech, and as nakedly intended for political consumption abroad —where, it must again be shouted loudly and in tones of horrified outrage, *the US government, under Mr Obama, is running cravenly apologetic telly adverts in Pakistan.*[45] It was craven, it was contemptible, and it should by rights lead either to Mr Obama's impeachment or to his defeat in November.

Yet it is applauded by far too many who ought, surely, to know better; and some of them, particularly in Mr Obama's imperial guard of a lapdog press, have exerted themselves to assist in it, as by identifying Mr Nakoula's residence for the convenience of the gentry in the bomb vests. (CNN has made a meal of posting the identifying personal information of a man who has not been charged with a crime and who is already the subject of death threats; yet if Mr Nakoula is to be reprehended for allegedly inciting those who then murdered Ambassador Stevens, which is the line CNN takes, then are not they accessories to any harm that befalls *him*?) This should surprise no one: Mr Holder's DOJ press office colludes regularly in planting stories in the press and dictating the spin to be given news, as in the collaborations of Ms Tracy Schmaler with the court eunuchs of Media Matters for America.

Mr Nakoula is not precisely Sir Salman Rushdie; but he shall be fortunate if he survives as long, and he is staring at the same fate *for the*

---

[44] We make quite certain that some Bright Spark in the Justice Department, having once seen *The Producers,* is hoping that Mr Nakoula employed the Bialystock & Bloom method of fund-raising and accounting. If so, that is one thing. But it is ridiculous, whatever the ground of his conviction, and at least *ought* to be unconstitutional, that he is barred from expressions of speech and opinion not related to his conviction or the acts that resulted in it.

[45] This seems imprudent as well as utterly contemptible. In the first place, the power's not on all that often in Pakistan. In the second, if these interrupt a cricket match on the telly, mobs shall take to the street and sack the US embassy.

same thought-crime. It's not as if the enemies of free speech are done with Sir Salman, after all: the bounty on his head has been increased, and his enemies are unrepentant even now. And of course Danish cartoonists and publishers, Dutch film-makers, and Dutch parliamentarians, have all seen what happens when one is accused of this thought crime: one may, sometimes, live, but one shall live thereafter in a cage —*with the approval and collusion of Leftist journalists, authors, and academics for the caging and the gaolers.*

And there is no statute of limitations, it appears, applicable to this thought-crime or any associated *fatwa.*

Yet there are those who ought to know better who have lined up under the banner of opposing free speech. Let us look, for example, at one Anthea Butler, an academic at the University of Pennsylvania. One should like very much to say that surely there can be no other person in any American university who should act so stupidly, but that's all too unlikely. We recognise that the professor shall quite likely object to having her actions and comments characterised as thick, unintelligent, and bleeding idiotic, but we make sure she should prefer to be regarded as having acted rather out of folly than from malice, and malignity is the only other possible explanation.

Professor Butler is a woman (of colour, as if that mattered a damn)[46] who teaches Religion at a coeducational institution; and her discipline is not apparently restricted to teaching a Salafist curriculum in Islam. *Politicised* Islam —Islamism rather than the religion itself —should, we make quite certain, consider this sufficient grounds to mark Professor Butler for the chop were they ever to be in a position to do so. Blithely unperturbed,

---

[46] As we shall shortly see, Identity Politics are a significant part of the problem, here.

Professor Butler's immediate reaction to the mobs' murderous rampages

was to tweet, *seriatim,*

> Good Morning. How soon is Sam Bacile going to be in jail folks? I
> need him to go now.[ ]When Americans die because you are
> stupid...
> And yes, I know we have First Amendment rights,[47][ ]but if you
> don't understand the Religion you hate, STFU about it. Yes, I am
> ticked off.—
> And people do [go] to jail for speech. First Amendment doesn't
> cover EVERYTHING a PERSON says.—
> I am all for free speech, but you better damn well understand that
> actions have consequences, and what you mock is another persons
> belief.—
> [T]he murder of the Ambassador and the employees is wrong,
> wrong. But Bacile will have to face his actions which he had
> freedom[48]—

after which, unrepentant, she (wait for it) penned an editorial for *USA
Today* in which she stated as follows (our remarks in bold):

> If there is anyone who values free speech, it is a tenured professor!

Evidently not.

> So why did I tweet that Bacile should be in jail? The "free speech"
>
> in Bacile's film is not about expressing a personal opinion about
>
> Islam.

How not? It seems to us that that is exactly what it was.

> It denigrates the religion by depicting the faith's founder in several
>
> ludicrous and historically inaccurate scenes to incite and inflame
>
> viewers.

Unfortunately (for Professor Butler), that is neither the legal nor the

philosophical standard for the protection of the right of free

---

[47] An assertion we beg leave to doubt. Her knowledge seems superficial at best in this area.

[48] No, we've no idea what she's trying to say, either, any more than do you. Or she.

expression and the publication of one's views.

> Bacile's movie is not the first to denigrate a religious figure, nor will it be the last. *The Last Temptation of Christ* was protested vigorously. The difference is that Bacile indirectly and inadvertently inflamed people half a world away, resulting in the deaths of U.S. Embassy personnel.

Precisely. **Curious how the protests in Christendom resulted in no deaths. Certainly that is a difference. But look at Professor Butler's next assertion: that 'Bacile *indirectly and inadvertently* inflamed people half a world away'. One could stop there. Even were the film to constitute incitement within the meaning of the law, and in such a way as to justify a restraint upon speech, its having 'incited' distant viewers '*indirectly and inadvertently*' ends the enquiry and resolves the question in Mr Nakoula's favour. Full sodding stop.**

> Bacile's movie does not excuse the rioting in Libya and Egypt, or the murder of Americans. That is deplorable.

This is the only worthwhile statement the professor has made to date, and it ought to have been the entirety of her editorial.

> Unfortunately, people like Bacile and Terry Jones, the Florida pastor who provoked international controversy by burning copies of the Quran, have a tremendous impact on religious tolerance and U.S. foreign policy.

And? What of it? Citizens seeking by free expression to influence the policy of their own government are engaged in the most jealously protected speech known to the solicitude of the law: *political* speech. If there *is* any category of speech that is and ought to be more sedulously

protected than political speech, in fact, it is Terry Not-the-Python Jones' speech, which is *religious* speech.

> Case in point: Gen. Martin Dempsey, chairman of the Joint Chiefs
> of Staff, called Jones on Wednesday to ask him to stop promoting
> Bacile's film. Clearly, the military considers the film a serious threat
> to national security. If the military takes it seriously, there should
> be consequences for putting American lives at risk.

This is gobsmackingly stupid. Governmental restraint upon protected speech is bad enough to deserve outrage. Deploying *the military against protected domestic speech* ought to bring a government down overnight. Christ, the Left haven't shut up about Vietnam since it started; if this is now their principle, *everything* has been reversed: the World Turn'd Upside-Down, as performed at Yorktown. You know, we were wrong just now: this is not merely stupid; this is an outrage. Accept this principle, and the Obama administration, merely for its political convenience, had been authorised to tell (well, *try* to tell, and best of British luck with *that*) the late Marie Colvin not to go to Syria and to keep shtum on the whole boiling. General Dempsey, for his part, ought to do the only honourable thing and resign his commission immediately; if he does not, he should face a court of enquiry at the very least, and quite possibly a court-martial.

> While the First Amendment right to free expression is important,
> it is also important to remember that other countries and cultures
> do not have to understand or respect our right.

Balls. So far, we have restrained ourselves to using the word, 'rubbish', when what we mean is 'balls' (or, in American, 'horseshit'), but our patience is exhausted. They mayn't want to understand it, but they

damned well want to respect it, *or be compelled to do so.*

This is not, at least, craven, nor malign: there is that to be said for it. It is merely unutterably stupid (we shan't descend to the level of Professor Butler's tweet that, if she doesn't understand the law and the rights at issue, she should shut the fuck up about them). For malignity in the universities, we must, alas, turn to St Antony's Oxon.[49]

Oxford, that notable home to lost causes, is home to one Faisal Devji, University Reader in Modern South Asian History and Fellow of St Antony's College, Oxford, and one Ms Sharmine Narwani, a Senior Associate Member —in effect, a junior research fellow, more or less —at St Antony's.

A few days ago —14 September 2012 —Dr Devji was amongst those contributing to a retrospective in the *Grauniad* upon the controversy that surrounded the publication of *The Satanic Verses*. He regards it as the beginning of global Muslim mobilisation against 'insults against Muhammad' and of their expressing 'their feelings of outrage at [Rushdie's] depiction of Muhammad, [expressed] by using the secular language of libel, defamation and hate speech'; and he so regards it *with approbation*. He goes on to make the breathtakingly objectionable statement, 'But even after other such controversies, over cartoons or papal comments, all concerned with insults against Muhammad, debate about them is dominated by *old-*

---

[49] It is Mr Wemyss' view that St Antony's has now succeeded LSE as the institution making the running in trading scholarship – and academic freedom – in exchange for students from abroad at so many petrodollars a head. It is also Mr Wemyss' view that this is a shame: one didn't actually *know,* when one was up, any Tantony Pigs, as one knew chaps at Univ or Oriel or Worcester or Trinity, or had connexions at Exeter, or, if in want of rough trade, might just consider tricking with Balliol or Wadham sorts if they *washed* first, but it's still rather a disgrace to have an Oxford college behaving in this fashion. Mr Wemyss is at least unfeignedly thankful that no one at the House seems to be of this kidney.

fashioned ideas about free expression. Confined as they legally are to individual countries, *such ideas have no standing in the global arena where these controversies occur'* [emphasis damned well added].

And then there is Ms Narwani, who has publicly expressed herself upon the mob's murder of Ambassador Stevens in Benghazi. She relieved herself of the following thoughts on Twitter:

> 100s of 1,000s of Arabs & Muslims slaughtered by American troops. Tell me again why I should care about whatshisname-plus-three?
> Oh do stop yr whining just b/c I'm not crying over a white guy who died in the line of duty. Tell it to all the dead brown mamas.
> —
> Hussein, what would a House Arab like yourself who backs senseless US wars against Arabs know about being human?—[50]

There is really only one thing to say about these views, Ms Narwani's, Dr Devji's, and Professor Butler's: they are perfectly entitled to hold and express these views. And *we* are wholly entitled —and quite right —to note that they are profoundly unscholarly views to hold, to hold them in contempt, and to hold them out for public mockery.

That is the problem: the problem with the Left, with these academics, with hacks such as Mr Rose, with journalists who are willing slaves to politicians, and with the demagogic politicians themselves —and of course, and above all, with the murderous and fanatical mobs, of any description, who insist upon a heckler's veto and transform it into a terrorist's veto. All those who would carve out from the realm of free speech, exceptions for what *they* declare to be 'hate speech', and all who, like Ms Narwani, have

---

[50] It is just as well Ms Narwani is at St Antony's, not at Wolfson. Wolfson's motto is taken from Terence's splendid line, *Homo sum: humani nil a me alienum puto:* a proposition with which Ms Narwani evidently does not concur. (For the benefit of Cambridge graduates and others bereft of Latin, we construe as follows: 'I am a man; I consider that nothing human is foreign to me.')

found in Identity Politics an excuse for suppressing free expression and applauding or at best dismissing murders committed —by their own lights and their own assertions —in that suppression, are the enemies not only of the freedom to speak and the freedom to publish, but, ultimately, of the freedom to think. There is no greater *trahison des clercs.*

The common thread

In late July, shortly before he ended up in hospital, Mr Pyle was confronting enemies of free speech: secular, political enemies of free speech and the freedom to publish. Mr Wemyss has been attempting to convey these principles in a colloquy on Twitter. Mobs have rioted across the Muslim world, and diplomats have been slain, allegedly because Muhammad was 'insulted' in a film clip on YouTube. Western governments and public figures have shown themselves shaky reeds indeed in responding, or failing to respond, to these events abroad with a full-throated defence of free speech, even, indeed especially, where one disagrees with or despises the speech or the speaker: for, after all, it costs nothing to defend polite, non-controversial speech. The bounty for the assassination of Sir Salman Rushdie has been increased; Mr Nakoula has been enthusiastically made a target for the next murderer, with the avid complicity of the Obama administration and much of the US press. Mr Kimberlin has waged lawfare against his critics. Mr Rose and many others wish to punish and to silence any opinions that do not comport with theirs, including by striking at academic freedom. Censorship has found a defender in an Ivy League professor of religion, who wishes to subcontract the restraint of protected speech *in America* to the US military. A Fellow at St Antony's Oxon believes that free speech is an old-fashioned idea confined to certain countries, and having no standing in the global arena; another academic at the same college is so wrapt in Identity Politics as to believe that she need not condemn a mob or a murder so long as the mob and the murderers were her own people, even if the effect —perhaps *specially* if the effect —is to chill free speech in free nations.

The Left in America have, as Professor Althouse and Professor Reynolds have noted, joined the Obama administration in asserting that corporations are not 'persons' in law;[51] with, as Professor Althouse wisely points out, the corollary that they must not be allowed freedom of speech, and above all that they not be allowed freedom to engage in *political* speech.[52]

There have been straws in the wind well before now. On a Bank Holiday Monday in 2005, an Oxford undergraduate named Sam Brown (a Balliol man. Bless. Poor thing) jocularly (after, no doubt, some jars of jolly-juice) asked a policeman —not a proctor —'Do you know your horse is gay? I hope you're comfortable riding a gay horse'; for which he was dragged down the nick and got a touch of £80 for his 'offence'. Worse yet, the police spokesthug stated that these allegedly 'homophobic'[53] remarks offended *or had the potential to offend* 'the policeman *and his horse*' as well as 'any members of the general public in the area.'[54]

---

[51] We shall believe that bodies corporate – *including newspapers and trades unions* – do not enjoy legal personhood only when they cease to be able to enter into contracts, sue, *be sued, and be prosecuted for violations of law*. If that is the brave new world the Left seeks, then on their own – often unionised – heads, and the heads of the Leftists in the press thus deprived of the the right to endorse candidates and unionists who can no longer keep Labour afloat, be it.

[52] The Left in America is willing to crawl through any sewer and abandon any principle to see the back of *Citizens United*.

[53] Mr Wemyss states that, although he cannot speak for, say, Mr Dale, Mr Tatchell, Mr Boles, Mr Duncan, Mr Laws, Mr Fry, or Lord Mandelson, and shouldn't care to do on a bet, it is his view that he and other gay subjects of the Crown really aren't such delicate flowers as to be in want of protection from undergraduate humour.

[54] There is no evidence that there *were* any offended members of the general public, or indeed any members of the Great British Public present at all. Only an utter horse's arse could utter the po-

It's amusing, in a morbid way; *but it is absolutely to be understood that if you live in a country with 'hate speech' laws, you are not free.* If a pissed-as-a-newt Balliol undergraduate can be banged up in gaol and fined £80 for calling a *horse* 'gay', *the UK is no longer a free country.* Never mind Milton, we want an AP Herbert now, with his *Misleading Cases:* this is straight out of *R v Haddock:* 'It cannot be too clearly understood that this is *not* a free country, and it will be an evil day for the legal profession when it is. The citizens of London must realize there is almost nothing they are allowed to do. People must not do things for fun. There is no reference to fun in any Act of Parliament.' The only distinction of course being that what was hilarious as fiction is an outrage in fact.

Straws in a black and bitter wind. And those straws, in that wind, yet blow about: Chris Matthews thinks it somehow 'arrogant' of Mitt Romney to stand for election against Mr Obama: presumably, Mr Obama should be re-elected without opposition.

A councillor in the California town of San Bernardino, a Mr Chas Kelly, sought to have a citizen prosecuted for telling him that he'd face a recall election if he voted against a certain measure.

The Egyptian government seeks the extradition of Terry Jones and Mr Nakoula and company to face capital charges.

The SPLC continues to draw up lists of 'hate groups' without any scholarly or professional expertise or qualification that might suggest they have a competence to do so, and manage to have them taken seriously (when Eugene Genovese is placed in the same category as Ernst Zundel and

---

faced idiocy that the *horse* was potentially offended. The Left, which cherishes the idea if not the reality of themselves At the Barricades, really wants to think about how – *and against whom* – the illiberal measures it is shrieking for should in fact be enforced.

Fred Phelps, and when Gary W Gallagher —*fifteen years ago* —was forced to defend himself pre-emptively against charges of being a 'Neo-Confederate', something has an ancient and fish-like smell).

Channel Four has knuckled under to threats and taken Tom Holland's documentary on Islam and its origins off the air, although it can be viewed on the Net.

Yale, you will recall, in 2009, put out a book about the Danish cartoons from which it excised, by way of a sort of pre-emptive self-censorship, all depictions of Muhammad —including the cartoons that were its subject.

Or consider this unnerving straw in a wind from an unexpected quarter. One of the few things that can and does move *bien-pensant* Western 'Useful Idiots' to criticise the despots of the PRC, is China's oppression of Tibet. The same crowd of muesli-munching Seekers, humming Three Dog Night's 'Shambala' all the while, have a romantic view of Nepal as well. (Mr Wemyss simply has a sound appreciation of the virtues and martial qualities of the Brigade of Gurkhas, and a deep sadness at what is happening to Nepal nowadays. Bloody Communists.) Yet the Westerners flicking their lighters to Bob Seger's 'Kathmandu' have perhaps never heard of Manish Harijan, the artist, and the Siddhartha Art Gallery, where freedom of expression is even now being stomped upon with jackboots by the Kathmandu District Administration Office (DAO) in Nepal. Mr Harijan has received death threats for daring to paint and to display paintings in which the Hindu gods are re-imagined, their new avatars in his art borrowing from the iconography of such Western comic-book figures as Ghost Rider and Superman. The Siddhartha Art Gallery, for mounting an exhibition of these works, has been sealed by the DAO.

What is the common thread here?

One strand is fear. Not the understandable fear of attack from abroad (it is in the fevered dreams of the *Left* that Muslims are regarded as an undifferentiated and bestial mass of savages coming to conquer and to kill: savages and children incapable of being reasoned with, of obeying the dictates of right reason, and of comporting themselves in conformity to a universal moral standard: it was amongst Said's allies, if anywhere, that the 'orientalism' which Said believed himself to have discovered, resided);[55] nor the ignoble but comprehensible fear of social or political or economic ostracism: rather, it is the fear of debate itself.

It is the fear of debate. It is the fear of being forced to *think*.

Recall Mr Rose: 'FUCK YOU! FUCK YOU! FUCK YOU FOR WRITING THAT YOU HAVEN"T SEEN ANY EVIDENCE[56].... OUR RIGHTS ARE NOT FOR AN ASSHOLE LIKE YOU TO DEBATE.'

Recall Professor Butler: 'And yes, I know we have First Amendment rights,but if you don't understand the Religion you hate, STFU [Shut The Fuck Up] about it.'

You, being sane, will naturally ask, Who can be afraid of debate? What's the worst that can happen? You lose a debate?

Ah. We'll get to that in a moment.

Recall, please, Ayatollah Hassan Sanei and his clown posse: the latest pretext for riot and murder 'won't be the last insulting act as long as Imam Khomeini's historic order on executing the blasphemous Salman Rushdie is

---

[55] Were this true, of course, honourable, devout Muslims in Libya should not have – as they have done – apologised to the US for the acts of their compatriots *and attacked the Islamist militia and its leaders who are responsible for the murders at the Benghazi consulate.*

[56] Imagine: a man trained as a lawyer asking for evidence. Shocking of Mr Pyle to do so. (He didn't make much of a fist of *being* a lawyer, did our Mr P, but *some* of the training did stick, after all.)

not carried out. If the imam's order [had been] carried out, the further insults in the form of [the Danish] caricatures, articles, and films would not have taken place. The impertinence of the grudge-filled enemies of Islam, which is occurring under the flag of the Great Satan, America, and the racist Zionists, can only be blocked by the absolute administration of this Islamic order.'

Why are the successors in courage of Oriana Fallaci and Theo van Gogh: the Ayaan Hirsi Alis, the Ahmed Aboutalebs, the Ibn Warraqs and Magdi Allams, the Fiamma Nirensteins and Caroline Fourests, the Robert Redekers, and far too many more beside: now familiar with life under police protection? Why does Kurt Westergaard have a panic room? Why was BHL —Bernard-Henri Lévy —targeted for assassination?

Why was Orhan Pamuk tried? What motivates idiots who embarrass the name of 'Christian' to burn books, or indeed to seek to ban them?

Why was Farag Foda murdered? Why was Naguib Mahfouz wounded in an assassination attempt?

And why is Mr Harijan under threat in Kathmandu, where Buddhism and Hinduism are the majority religions and the new national Nepali government is deeply in thrall to Maoists, who at least are meant to be *atheists*?

These are not all instances of Islamist violence and intolerance: that is the point. Leftist secular intolerance, fundamentalist Prot intolerance, intolerance in Oriental religions, ultra-nationalism, and what can only be called intolerance in the service of a politicised view of gay rights,[57] are all

---

[57] Mr Wemyss wishes it to be clearly understood that at least gay political extremism is, as against the others, fabulously dressed, is devastatingly fashionable, has *much* better music, and knocks off early for drinks.

implicated.

Think back to Ms Narwani: 'Tell me again why I should care...? Oh do stop [your] whining just [because] I'm not crying over a white guy who died in the line of duty. Tell it to all the dead brown mamas. Hussein, what would a House Arab like yourself[,] who backs senseless US wars against Arabs[,] know about being human?'

It is the end and aim and purpose, not merely the effect, of Identity Politics, and of the assertion of a purported countervailing 'right' not to be offended, to render the rights of free thought, and of speech and expression and publication of one's thoughts, no longer universal; to render them restricted to favoured groups, and bestowed, not as rights but as privileges, by the State: either *en bloc* to members of favoured groups, or piece-meal to applicants from non- or disfavoured groups. In short, the intended purpose of these constructs is to make rights no longer rights, but privileges, bereft of universality.

The motivating fear that drives this embrace of tyranny is the fear of debate. The fear is the fear that comes of knowing that, if it comes to debate, one is forced to examine, to confront, and to *think*.

How do we know that an idea is false, or that a play is no bloody good, or that a poem is appallingly bad? How are we to know that a proposition is or is not sound, or a custom or a law bad or corrupted or otherwise in want of repeal or reform? A man who is wrong about one thing, even a very important thing, may not be wrong in all things; but again, he may: his false principles and consequent false dealings may be such that he cannot be trusted with a fiver, a bottle of singlemalt, a housemaid, or to give an honest answer to the question, What day of the week is it. How shall we know what he is wrong about, and how far wrong, and why, and if he is indeed wrong, and how far he can be trusted if it all?

Obviously, the idea, the proposition, the painting or the prose, the criticism, the censure, the falsehood and the truth, must first be uttered, freely and without reservation or censorship —including self-censorship. It must then be debated: freely and without reservation or censorship — including self-censorship.[58] And *that* is what threatens unto panic the Kimberlins and the Roses, the ayatollahs Sanei and the professors of all descriptions, the swivel-eyed Islamists and the swivel-eyed Southern Baptists, the Turkish nationalists, the police art critics of Kathmandu, and the secular True Believers in one or another ism.

One might think that the blatant hypocrisy of demanding, particularly on the Left, Free Speech for Me But Not For Thee, could not be borne even by those making the demands; that the internal contradictions of the position, the sheer weight of hypocrisy, should become insupportable even to those putting the hypocritical demands forward. And it is quite likely that the spin Dr Devji and Professor Butler employ, that a universal right is 'merely a Western construct', like the Identity Politics to which Ms Narwani and Mr Rose resort, is a psychological necessity to allow them to persist in their inherently self-refuting beliefs and demands.

This may be so.[59] Yet what we must acknowledge now is that all wars are wars of religion. The wars of the last century were wars of religion: the Great War, a war of the debased religion of nationalism; the Hitler War, a

---

[58] This, by the way, is one very good reason why we do not and should never say to Professor Butler that, when she comments upon law, policy, and political philosophy she doesn't understand, she should shut up (note absence of expletives). She should speak; *and she should then be prepared to defend her views in open and honest debate.* And lose gracefully when she does.

[59] Or as Mr Wemyss prefers to put it, 'You might very well think that; I couldn't *possibly* comment.'

war of bastardised religion in the form of ideologies that had become ideolatries; the Cold War and its hot passages at arms, the same. The current struggles, in whatever form, from shouting matches in the opinion columns of broadsheets to actual combat in deserts and waste places, are the same again, the mixture as before: and the religions that are locked in struggle are not Islam and Christianity (and secularism), but rather ideologies given *latria,* worship, cult, of which Islamism, *politicised* Islam, happens currently to make one.

Wars, far more than politics, make strange bedfellows, dubious alliances. The rationally-inexplicable embrace by the Left of Islamism, or at least of its objectives and its perceived utility to the Leftist cause, is explicable when this fact is acknowledged: like Stalin, the Left of today is perfectly content to ally with fascism to carve up one territory, and then to run after what aid it can find from the enemies of fascism when that ravening maw is turned upon the Left's own tender flesh. And although this is typical of the Left, it is not unknown on the Right: hard as it may be to conceive now, there was a time when Tipper Gore and her senatorial then-husband tried mightily to ride a wave of moral panic ... to the fabled shore of censoring rap music and its lyrics. (These are, unquestionably, often offensive, misogynistic, violent, and hateful; they are not infrequently vile, base, and contemptible;[60] but they are protected speech, and either you believe in free speech or you don't.) It's all a matter of whose ox is being gored:[61] in warfare, it is a common delusion, only temporarily and sporadically true, that the enemy of my enemy is my friend.

---

[60] As opposed to viol, bass, and continuo. On the other hand, 'Vile, Base & Contemptible' really does make a great name for a band.

[61] Or in the case of Tipper's ex-husband, that greenery-yallery ex-pol turned celeb filmmaker, whose Gore is being asked.

All wars are wars of religion: the current culture wars, as they are somewhat dubiously called, included. It is as true now as it was when GKC and Jack Lewis and K Clark were pointing it out by way of reminder to a Whiggishly-educated public that had been encouraged to forget it, that the *dulia,* not *latria,* that was given to the BVM in the High and Late Middle Ages, was of a particular quality that meant that, when the reformers accused Roman Catholic Christians of Mariolatry, and in reaction denigrated the Virgin, men felt as if their mothers or sisters or daughters had been attacked. And reacted accordingly. It is no less true that Islamism makes cynical political use of the Muslim veneration for Muhammad, as it has been notably doing in the past fortnight, and that the regard in which Muslims who are not at all themselves Islamists do hold Muhammad, is, in feeling, similar to the *dulia* that Roman Christianity grants the Blessed Virgin.

Now extend your horizons. Concede, as we think one must, that what wracks and roils the world today is a conflict of ideologies that have taken on many or all of the attributes of religion. Consider that the secular Left, the academy, the practitioners of Identity Politics —be those politics Islamism, pan-Arabism, gay politics and the burning desire to get same-sex marriage through by any means, irredentist Turkish nationalism, anti-'orientalism', racial or religious solidarity, or what have you —and all the rest of those we've surveyed, are invested in their causes even as devout believers are invested in their faiths. Mr Rose, for example, has clearly lost his very sense of self in his cause; Ms Narwani has desensitised herself to human sympathy in hers; Professor Butler has suffered a serious case of *déformation professionnelle.* Journalists and writers have abandoned the very principles of their professions for political reasons. And why?

Because they fear debate. Opposition must be silenced, delegitimised, marginalised; academic freedom must be sued out of existence if necessary; dissent must not be allowed: for if these things are not done, there shall be debate. And that must not be allowed.

Why must it not be allowed? What is the worst that can happen? Why do they proclaim a right not to be offended that, they claim, trumps the universal human right to think and speak and publish freely?

Because their entire sense of self, their concept of themselves, their souls and identities, are wholly subsumed in their chosen causes, faiths, and identities. And if such a person should chance to be challenged, to be made to reflect, to be forced to self-examination —if such a one were defeated in debate, as he should be were he to permit debate —it is not his or her cause or opinions, his or her *Weltanschauung* or the *Weltansicht* of his or her affinitive or elective community, that is shattered: it is himself or herself. Its is indeed his or her *self*. A psychologically intolerable shattering occurs, far beyond mere cognitive dissonance that can be rationalised; the insupportable prospect of their own mortality and impotence threatens, self-esteem is swept away, and all the cunning devices of terror management fail at once and catastrophically. Rather than this, for such persons, anything: the betrayal of principle; the abandonment of intellectual honesty: *nothing* is too base to be seized upon as a means of holding back that disintegrating realisation. Fear is one thing: it can be rationalised or overcome; this, however, is the unmanning prospect of existential angst as Kierkegaard knew and described it. To fend that off, people resort without shame to any means, however low, and sacrifice anyone and anything they must. And *because* they are True Believers —persons whose entire sense of self, and self-worth and self-esteem, is bound inextricably to and subsumed in their Cause —they can rationalise even this: for the Cause is Just, and the end is self-evidently Noble, and all means are worthy in such a Cause. The Islamists and Salafists of today, exploiting the devotion of Muslims of whom they themselves are the leading killers, have seized upon this, this binding of the self to the faith and the community, the *ummah*, this loss of selfhood in a greater cause; the persons who have ranged themselves in the ranks fighting against free speech and free expression are no different, at once the exploiters and the sufferers of this stifling fear that one inconvenient fact, one scholarly article, one book, one play, one painting, one lost debate, should forever destroy the worldview that has become their world and their very self. It doesn't matter if the Cause in which their individuality has been allowed to dissolve be same-sex marriage, anthropogenic global warming, or the heckler-cum-terrorist's veto: what matters is that they cannot allow free and open debate upon it, for if it perchance fail that test, they are in their own eyes as good as dead, their souls destroyed with the cause in which they have placed them.

One can pity such people, and hope for their healing. But they stand as an awful warning against the perils of allowing oneself to be corrupted thus even in the best of causes and with the best of intentions; and they certainly mustn't be allowed further, corrupting power as arbiters of what free men and women may and may not think and say and publish. They of all people must not sit in judgement upon free speech. They would have you believe, for their own comfort, that some speech that is properly and rightly protected *must not be allowed.*

That they are mistaken is one thing. That their motives are what they are is another. And both these things are immaterial. What matters is what they believe and are straining to do: and it is *that* – their aim, not their motive or their pathology: *what they mean to do, not what they believe* – is what cannot and must not be allowed.

Anyone who palliates violence; who seeks to carve out exceptions, beyond those recognised at the beginning of this paper, to your freedoms; who seeks to persuade you that they have a 'right' not to be offended; who in any way asserts the right to fetter your freedom to think and say and publish as you like: is an enemy of freedom. He is your enemy; she would be your tyrant. Such persons are on the same moral level as al-Qaeda or a terror-supporting imam, if not lower: and they are infinitely more dangerous. By all lawful means, and at all costs however high, you must resist them, debate them, force them to debate you, and show them up for what they are. You must defend even those speakers and views you yourself disdain and despise, for the sake of the principle. Or you shall deserve the servitude and slavery that shall be your portion under those who pretend to be your censors and seek to be your masters —if they allow you to live at all.

For the past fortnight has shown once more the fatal consequences of Danegeld and appeasement, even as the greatest of writers and painters turned statesman once thundered:

> ... the terrible words have for the time being been pronounced against the Western democracies: 'Thou art weighed in the balance and found wanting.' And do not suppose that this is the end. This is only the beginning of the reckoning. This is only the first sip, the first foretaste of a bitter cup which will be proffered to us year by year *unless by a supreme recovery of moral health and martial vigour, we arise again and take our stand for freedom as in the*

olden time.

Arise, then, and stand with us for freedom, whilst yet we may.

Augury: What we foresaw in the 2012 US elections (and, lo, it did come to pass):
3 November 2012:

> *If Mr Wemyss is depressed beyond measure by having foreseen all too clearly where the UK's political threats to press freedom tended, Mr Pyle is grimly resigned to having descried – and decried – what Mr Obama should, in broad outline, do were the American electorate such fools as to re-elect him. He did not foresee and could not foresee just how bad it was to be. He certainly failed to foresee quite how spineless a second Obama administration should be abroad, or how complaisant at home with those who hate and fear free speech.*

Declaring an interest

We begin by Declaring an Interest. We are authors and publishers who do business in the United States as well as in the United Kingdom, the EU, and the world at large. Mr. Pyle is an American, a —some would say, "nominal" —Democrat, and what is called a "conservative" above all party labels (meaning that he is a Classical Liberal of the school of Hayek and Mises). Mr. Wemyss is equally a Gladstonian Liberal, which is why he is perforce a supporter of the Conservative Party (David Cameron notwithstanding). Being wiser than the average *Guardian* hack,[62] Mr. Wemyss considers it no business of his to tell Americans how to vote, and for whom, in what are, after all, their own country's elections. This is Mr. Pyle's paper in most regards. Nevertheless, it's neither unfair nor yet meddlesome to point out a few things about foreign trade and foreign affairs, the Special Relationship and NATO, and Mr. Wemyss has been encouraged to put points to Mr. Pyle that have influenced and informed this Paper, in the conclusions of which Mr. Wemyss wholly concurs.

The issues before the American electorate
Foreign affairs, intelligence, and defense

☐   Obama

√   Romney

The United States —even when not considered in light of its strategic partnership[63] with the United Kingdom, the Commonwealth (Australia, Canada, and India especially), the "Anglosphere" more generally, and its NATO allies —is the preponderant power in the world.

What is more, this is a *good* thing. No other power on the immediate horizon, were it to attain a similar preponderance, would conduct its affairs so much to the benefit of the peace, security, and liberalization, indeed liberation, of the world, as does the United States of America.

---

[62] The *Grauniad,* you may recall, in 2004 gathered all its muesli-munching, sandalled idiots to write, unsolicited, to "swing voters" in Clark County, Ohio, imploring them, and quite often instructing them, to vote against W. The results were, firstly, some hilariously unprintable responses even from Democrats who supported John Kerry and, secondly, an increased margin for George W. Bush in his re-election bid.

[63] E.g., UKUSA, AUSCANNZUKUS, TTCP, ABCA, PJB (Defence), and the CCEB.

Its allies tend to punch above their weight in international affairs for several reasons: in the case of the United Kingdom, by having a highly professional Defence establishment in HM Forces, with airlift and power-projection capacity of the first rank, underpinned by superior state-of-the-art intelligence services; in the case of most American allies (including the UK), in possessing clearly defined national interests, at least regional power to protect those interests, considerable deterrent capability, sophisticated intelligence and counter-intelligence capacities, *and the Americans as allies*. Additionally, American power as enjoyed, maintained, and projected, is founded in American values; in consequence, there is a moral component to American power and American interests, and, America being a democracy founded upon specific ideals of liberty, an internal corrective against the misuse of American power.

The primary rivals and indeed enemies of the United States are also the enemies or unfriends of the United Kingdom, the Commonwealth, NATO, and liberal democracy generally. These presently consist primarily in non-state actors driven by Islamism;[64] Iran as the patron of those non-state actors, in pursuit of regional hegemony under the mask of piety; small-state and non-state actors motivated by resentment or rapacity;[65] organized transnational criminal gangs;[66] the few remaining communist states bar the

---

[64] That is, politicized Islam: not the religion as such, but its bastardization by pols on the make and wanna-be warlords.

[65] Notably in Central and South America, and unfortunately also in the ISI, which state-within-the-state is increasingly the *de facto* government of Pakistan; the Bolivarian Alliance for the Peoples of Our America (ALBA) – and what the Commonwealth countries that are in with that lot are thinking, God and the FCO alone know – is the primary source of enmity, it being largely a mask for Venezuelan, Bolivian, and Cuban mischief-making, along with the Argentine.

[66] It is worth noting, depressingly, that Iranian subversion is increasingly common in Central and South America; and that Los Zetas and Iran, the *New York Times* reported last year, conspired to assassinate the Saudi ambassador to the US and to bomb Saudi and Israeli diplomatic targets.

PRC;[67] the Russian Federation;[68] and the People's Republic[69] of China itself, regardless of its political ideology, as a mere matter of power politics.

Were any of these rivals to the United States to assume a position of equal or superior power to that of the US and its allies, the world would *not* be better off. To the contrary, and regardless of the subsequent outcome. China today, and the Russian Federation still more, is in the position of Japan some decades ago (when Americans were worried that Japan, simply through economic success, was on the verge of eclipsing and assuming American power): already at peak, and about to suffer hugely dislocating economic, demographic, cultural, and internal political crashes. None of the immediately-foreseeable rivals to the United States for hyper-power status would be "sweet, just, boyish masters;" and any of them would, in the moment of apparent victory, begin a series of hard landings —almost certainly accompanied by internal strife, the rise of angry young nationalists, and increased militarization (which no country save the United States has ever been able to afford to the degree necessary to achieve and retain hyper-power status) —economic implosion, and a last gasp of foreign, likely armed, adventurism to stave off disaster. Moreover, the PRC and the Russian Federation, which could plausibly, for a brief time and with ruinous effort and expenditures, challenge the US for dominance, are facing already demographic death-spirals, while the more fertile states and non-state actors could only assert themselves with *Western* technology and weapons of mass destruction.

The national interests of the United States and its allies are free trade,

---

[67] Notably North Korea (the 'DPRK') and Cuba.

[68] Rapidly sliding back into Stalinism.

[69] *Soi-disant.*

global security, and the spread of democracy; the national interests of their opponents, the contrary. This fact, and not puerile fantasies about Zionist plots and the Israel Lobby, is why Israel, and —when freed of such succubi as Syria and Hamas —Lebanon, are America's natural allies and strategic partners in the Middle East: as Turkey was and may be again when the Erdogan folly of flirtation with dreams of the caliphate and of riding the Islamist tiger is finally shattered.

Mr. Wemyss has said, many times, that

> There are two primary strains in the Conservative Party: grocers, and grandees. ... By 'grandees' and 'grocers', I am not referring to social class or any of that; nor do I refer to the Worshipful Company of Grocers, all cloves and camels. I refer rather to two fundamental positions within the Conservative Party, regardless of one's antecedents. ... A grandee Conservative sees the country as a village: a village of which he and his party, when in government, act the Squire. As the Squire, the grandee moves jovially amongst his tenants in their tied cottages, dispensing largesse and reproof.... There are two problems with this model. The first is that HMG is not the Squire and the subjects of the Crown are not the smocked tenantry of the government of the day. The second is that these principles —or instincts, as one can hardly call them principles — however different they may be to the fiercely held maxims of Labour old and new, lead in the end to the same statist solutions as those the Left proposes, and to accepting and 'managing' statism when a Conservative government succeeds a Labour one. It is the grocers who will always and rightly attempt to roll back the State and its reach in favour of liberty.

Governor Romney has not endeared himself to the Cameroon grandees of the present Conservative Party, and has, regrettably, been used by Boris Johnson as a figure for a self-and-Olympics-promoting Two Minutes' Hate. Nor is he regarded favorably by the professional politicians, ward-heelers, and placemen of the EU. This may not worry American voters unduly; it is nevertheless a fact.

Against that are numerous other facts.

President Obama, in his term, has openly rejected the Special Relationship, repeatedly insulted the Prime Minister when the PM was the Rt Hon. Gordon Brown, effectively sided with Argentina over the Falklands, and made more than his own share of protocol gaffes when in the UK.

President Obama did not quite pull a Suez over Libya, but his "leading from behind" in that "kinetic action" did not precisely advance American interests in Libya or constitute the sort of support to which HM Government and the French were as allies entitled. Moreover, it is by now nakedly evident that Mr. Obama had no plan whatever for what should happen afterward.

This was shown conclusively in Benghazi on 11 / 12 SEP 2012, the eleventh anniversary of 9/11, when Ambassador Chris Stevens and three other Americans were murdered by what was decidedly *not* a "spontaneous protest over a YouTube clip." Ambassador Stevens became the first US ambassador to be slain in the line of duty since "Spike" Dubs in Kabul in 1979, at the previous nadir of American power. What is more, President Obama and his administration have been consistently disingenuous over the matter, repeatedly asserting, until it became impossible any longer to deny the obvious, that the murder of four Americans at a US consulate had been unforeseeable, unforeseen, unwarned-against, impossible to stop, spontaneous, unconnected to the anniversary of 9/11, and the unfortunate result of a protest over a film. Having been thus economical with the truth,

President Obama thereupon attempted to deceive the American public over what he said and when he said it. In fact, in his remarks in the Rose Garden —before bugg[er]ing off to Vegas for a fundraiser, an activity which, with golf, has been his primary occupation in office —immediately after the premeditated attack upon the Benghazi consulate, Mr. Obama described the event as an "outrageous and shocking attack" and a "brutal act": he prefaced his denunciation of "this type of senseless violence" by saying, "Since our founding, the United States has been a nation that respects all faiths. *We reject all efforts to denigrate the religious beliefs of others.* But there is absolutely no justification to this type of senseless violence." It was only in the context of a *pro forma* recollection of the original 9/11 that he said, "No acts of terror will ever shake the resolve of this great nation, alter that character, or eclipse the light of the values that we stand for" —whereupon he then again designated the Benghazi attack, not as a terrorist act, but as "this terrible act."

The American people are perfectly capable of handling the truth —if they had a government capable of telling it.

President Obama and his administration are not capable of that. Or so the Mexican government says, and with cause, as we shall see.

President Obama has expected defense and intelligence cooperation from HM Governments in the UK, Canada, Australia, and New Zealand, while burning their agents, denigrating their assistance, insulting their head of state and heads of government, demanding unequal extradition, at least *attempting* to buy Russian amity with UK nuclear codes, ignoring their warnings, and allowing their physical and intelligence assets to be taken from unprotected American installations and control. In order to further this president's re-election narrative, allied lives (and agents) have been sacrificed: the physician whom the CIA and DoD used to track bin Laden was burnt and is in a Pakistani jail, at the dubious mercy of the ISI.

In Mexico and Central America, a staggering number of people are dead at the hands of narco-terrorists armed —for domestic US political reasons peculiar to Mr. Obama —by US weapons "walked" and then lost by the Obama administration, in the operation cynically called FAST AND FURIOUS: which did not in fact begin under, nor yet did it resemble programs begun under, the previous administration. And as with the Benghazi debacle — itself suspiciously like a gun-walking operation, to Syrian jihadists —the administration is concerned only to hide, deny, cover-up, deceive, and conspire to hide the truth both from Congress and the American people (and HM Government, for that matter, in the case of Benghazi).

Since Barack Obama became president of the United States, the enemies and unfriends of the US and its allies have been emboldened and not infrequently materially aided; US and Western interests, substantially degraded and impaired. Governor Romney is by no means a military or foreign affairs thinker, but presidents have people for that: the question is one of instinct and philosophy. In the final assay, the first duty of a head of government is to secure the safety of his nation. Not only has President Obama signally failed to do that, he seems materially indisposed to do that, and to regard that duty as beneath him. Certainly, by way of example, any man who believes, or professes to believe —particularly in light of the PLA Navy's acquisition of *Liaoning* (ex-*Varyag*) and further plans for CV construction, and the utility of naval assets in anti-terror and asymmetrical warfare operations —that USN CVs can operate with or without the support vessels of a CSG (previously CVBG); that SSKs, SSGs, SSNs, SSBNs, and SSGNs can project power over time without surface vessels; or that in any way the submarine and the aircraft carrier have rendered other vessels obsolete or unnecessary, has no business putting himself forward to become President of the United States and commander in chief of the armed forces thereof.

Mr. Romney is clearly the superior choice in this regard.

Economic stewardship and policy

☐   Obama

√   Romney

The United States economy remains, as it has remained for some centuries now, the most remarkable engine for the creation of wealth *for the poor and aspiring* that the world has ever known.

No credit for this is due to President Obama, whose administration has conclusively demonstrated that capitalism truly is idiot-proof.

The president's hand-picked "winners" in his rigged game of *crony* capitalism have established a record of their own: fraud, bankruptcy, and automobiles the batteries of which explode when wet. For resolving to end this particular waste of public monies alone, Governor Romney deserves to be elected president.

No US president seeking to play the thimble-rigged game of a directed economy is going to pick winners: that's not the point. The point and the question is, Why would any US president do this sort of thing?

This once more rests upon character and philosophy — and life experience. Any historian worth his dust —we're more notable for that than for salt —must be aware and must insist that no action results from and no actor is ever moved by a single motive. A group of motives can, however, be identified in Mr. Obama's case.

The President appears truly to believe what he has professed to believe, that "at some point, you" [NB: not he] "have made enough money," and that wealth must be redistributed as a matter of policy, *by* the government. *His* enlightened government. Of course, this credo combines a really nasty sense of unjustified moral arrogance with a profound pig-ignorance of basic economics; but if public choice theory in economics teaches us anything, it is that —as Mr. Madison well knew —pols and bureaucrats are no less self-interested than the average Joe: and, in fact, more so, by a long chalk. And Mr. Obama and the wing, his wing, currently in control of the Democratic Party, have a considerable interest in demographic slicing and dicing, robbing Peter to pay Paul, bribing fifty-percent-plus-one of the electorate with the wealth created by the 49.99%, and setting groups —encouraged to create identities *as* groups —one against the other. Mr. Obama's personal political interest is to encourage a dependent class of citizens and non-citizens, persons who are net dependents upon government largesse, who will support him because of *and partly out of the proceeds of* his redistributing, to them, the wealth created by the net-contributing residents and their companies and businesses. It is a long history of success in doing just that that has maintained the Labour Party in Britain in great stretches of England, Wales, and Scotland —and left the UK in its present fiscal straits.

Debt is the great threat to the United States, American power, and the happiness and security of American citizens. This is especially so to the extent that the debt is the product of unsustainable deficit spending.

In the United Kingdom, the Islington-and-Notting-Hill wing of the Conservative Party has happily accepted the cover of the Coalition to eschew making any actual cuts —although they are savaged just as much as they'd be if they did. Europe as a whole is equally unwilling to take its medicine. Hard landings —with likely (and likely unpleasant) —geopolitical consequences: irredentism, adventurism, revanchism, military irresponsibility, and internal friction: are inevitable in the former Soviet Union, Pakistan, some at least of the Gulf states, the Levant and North Africa, Latin America, and, especially, China, where the South China Sea is already a flashpoint.

President Obama, in addition to having personal political interests and an ideology that are predisposed to deficit spending and economic folly, has never done an honest day's work in his life, or held any job that would have taught him the economic realities. Governor Romney is not, it is true, precisely a small-town merchant or heartland farmer, but he is not, as the President is, an economic illiterate (and innumerate).

President Obama is addicted to social programs, deficit spending, an absurd degree of regulation, and a *bien-pensant* hostility to all capitalism save crony capitalism. But even that is not fully the point. Mr. Obama, elected in large measure because of dissatisfaction with the fiscal policies of Mr. Bush and the bailout of Wall Street, has doubled down on the failed aspects of those policies, including the bailout boogie (in this regard, his approach is very much the same as in —contrary to all his promises — increasing drone strikes, shutting down investigations into enhanced interrogation techniques, and *not* closing Gitmo). More than that, he used the fiscal crisis as an excuse to force through, at a time when his party also controlled the House as well as the Senate, hugely expensive, unsustainable, falsely-costed, and massively unpopular social welfare programs that only increased the deficit and further diminished growth. In the pursuit of ideology and partisan advantage, the President has promoted policies that have contributed to a recovery-that-wasn't and unemployment figures that shock the conscience.

And in three and a half years now, he has neither engaged Republican budget proposals nor submitted his own or had his Senate majority do so.

Nor will he detail in any way his actual intentions, economically, for a second term —almost certainly because to do so would guarantee he's not given one.

His attitude towards regulatory burdens and getting government out of the way of American ingenuity and accomplishment is notably demonstrated in his willingness to grant subventions to foreign governments and companies to drill for oil and gas while being openly bent on wrecking domestic US coal and petroleum production and transshipment —despite the obvious fact that many of the United States' diplomatic problems abroad, as well as threats to American prosperity at home, would vanish overnight as America approached energy independence.

At the same time, his administration as well as the Fed (and most other central banks) has pursued a savagely deflationary policy against a non-existent threat of inflation.

This, with the certainty of his addiction to spending and regulation, and the uncertainty of what further destruction he intends to visit upon the wealth-creating sectors of the economy, is the greatest threat of all. Business and household budgeting is —as is the Treasury's —frozen in a stasis of uncertainty.

The crisis is not one of monetary supply. It is not even one of credit. It is a crisis of *velocity*. Growth —and the tax revenues that are the proceeds of growth —is stifled by uncertainty and by this president's past record. The equation of exchange —the connection between the general price level that the market derives and the monetary policy that a government pursues —is simple: $MV = Py$. That is, the monetary supply, M, multiplied by V, velocity, the number of times in a year that the average buck turns over in final purchases, is equal to the general price level (P) times the real income of the economy, y (e.g., GDP / GNP). This is a useful formula for inflation measurement, but it also points to the bottleneck that has this country in a hole right now: velocity. No one who is not a fool or a government employee spends freely —creates the velocity that gives thrust and lift to get the economy airborne —in the atmosphere that this administration has created and seems to be proud of. Even if the market might prefer another set of plans to those of the Romney-Ryan campaign, *any* plan is preferable to *no* plan, or a refusal to tell the public the plan until after the election.

Governor Romney wins this, hands down.

Domestic policy

☐ Obama

√ Romney

W hen all is said and done, the basic freedoms that the United States and her citizens enjoy are clearly set out in the Constitution, and not even the Supreme Court can long deny or interpret them away. The American people are not supine. This does not mean that the next round of Supreme Court appointments won't be important. Additionally, persons of good will can legitimately disagree both upon measures and policies, and upon the weight and importance to be given to these.

Quite frankly, when the American primary author of this paper sees, as he has seen in the past year, "activists" shrieking that their pet cause —say, "marriage equality" (that being the Orwellian label used by advocates of extending the legal bundle of rights and responsibilities, evolved over centuries of legislation and the common law and called "marriage," to partners of the same sex)[70] or "reproductive rights" (Newspeak for abortion, for taxpayer funding thereof, and for forcing poor people to pay for the contraceptives of upper-middle-class professional students) —he feels rather as he does when he hears of the "obesity epidemic among the poor." Are these issues deserving of careful consideration? Certainly. Are these "First World problems"? Oh, *hell* yes. When your poor are fat rather than starving, your country is rich indeed. When you have leisure to worry about

---

[70] The authors support civil unions *where these have been enacted by the people and their elected representatives rather than by judicial* ukase.

these issues, you have solved the graver and more immediate issues.

And America has *not* "solved the graver and more immediate issues" — not for sour apples, we haven't.

Governor Romney does not appear to be a wild-eyed ideologue; if there is an ideologue in this race, it is President Obama. And the tea-partisan tendency in his party is very adamantly not interested in social issues right now, save as they cause social programs and spending on social programs. The economic crisis, which also hampers the projection of America's military and diplomatic power, is by far the most important issue.

But if there are issues of rights and freedoms that are explicit in the Constitution, universally acknowledged by Americans, and currently under threat — and there are — they are threatened by Mr. Obama, his administration, and their mindset. The Leftist philosophy of cut-rate academics is hostile to free speech —see our prior Position Paper —and this administration, particularly when it invokes the false gods of "hating 'hate speech' and not tolerating intolerance," when it asserts that "the future mustn't belong to those who insult the prophet of Islam," and when it calls for restrictions upon free speech and free publication, is a government of cut-rate academics, by cut-rate academics, and for cut-rate academics, that really must soon perish from the earth. The foundational principle of American freedom can pretty well be expressed by saying that the future had damned well *better* belong to those who are *free* to insult the prophet of Islam, the Blessed Virgin, Our Savior, Moses, the Buddha, Vishnu, Richard Dawkins, and anyone else an American damned well pleases. And this government of cut-rate academics is as hostile to the free exercise of religion (save for those who *revere* the prophet of Islam) as it is to free speech.

Mr. Pyle is —like Mr. Wemyss, and with apologies to Will Rogers —not a member of any organized religion: he's an Anglican. And Mr. Pyle freely confesses that his opinion of Mr. Romney's religion is adequately summed up by the statement that he is hard pressed to remember to put the second "m" in "Mormon." But this is about an American election, and he takes as his text the only holy writ that matters: Article VI, the third paragraph, "no religious test shall ever be required as a qualification to any office or public trust under the United States." Here endeth the lesson.

Governor Romney may, as he is free to do, believe any number of damned-fool things; President Obama does, as the irreverend Rev. Mr. Wright's theology demonstrates. Of the two, perhaps Governor Romney is more likely to pursue religious indifference in government, as members of off-brand religions are wont to do. But in any case, it is abundantly clear which of these men is worthier of our trust as a defender of explicit constitutional freedoms, and it is *not* the trimming, apologizing Mr. Obama.

And it is likewise evident that President Obama, as a Leftist ideologue — indeed, idolater —in a second term with no re-election to concern himself with,[71] is far likelier to meddle with non-essential domestic issues (and implicating acknowledged rights) than is Mr. Romney, who grasps the essential truth that free contraceptives paid for by the Federal government are meaningless even were they desirable *if the government goes broke while everyone farts around fighting a* Kulturkampf.

---

[71] After all, this is the very suspicion as to *foreign* affairs that inevitably arises from his incautious remarks to Mr. Medvedev about "flexibility" after the election.

President Obama began his term by choosing to drop a civil rights case —
for voter suppression, against the New Black Panthers —*that DoJ had
already won in a default judgment.* His Department of Justice and his
Attorney General have become notorious for the naked partisanship with
which they prosecute and defend, or decline to prosecute or to defend, the
laws, and violations of those laws. Perfunctory defenses of statutes the
constitutionality of which has been challenged and which do not reflect an
administration's philosophy —a failing sadly not confined to any one
president, party, or administration —has given way to wholesale refusal even
to go through the motions (and briefs, and pleadings.... Sorry. Lawyer
humor). And the twin — and dangerous — tendencies of the Obama
administration in the law have been an ever-increasing reliance upon
regulation, *ukase,* executive order, and, frankly, rule by decree, coupled with
an overtly partisan issuance of waivers, exceptions, protections, opt-outs,
and loopholes to and in favor of favored groups, loyal cronies, ward-heelers,
rent-seekers, and campaign contributors.

The Obama administration habitually exercises its legal discretion to
grant states a pass on not getting ballots to American servicemen, while
taking a laissez-faire approach to voter fraud that shades into open hostility
towards any attempt to prevent it.

The Obama administration is hostile to the exercise of unquestioned
constitutional rights of free speech and free exercise *even as it engages in
attempting to create new "rights" taken from Leftist legal theory.*

The Obama administration, in sum —and in contrast to Governor
Romney's executive record —is actually a peculiarly lawless one, in that it is

inimical to the rule of law, partisan in applying the law, and increasingly inclined to ignore the law as written for political advantage and the pursuit of favoritism. There are as always many motives for this, some or most of which might separately seem harmless and indeed amiable, but which together mean simply a preference for the rule of party and partisanship in place of the equal and detached enforcement of the laws as they stand, laws passed by the representatives of the people.

And this is of a piece with the Obama administration's overall record. President Obama promised fundamentally to transform the United States. Unfortunately, he seems to have meant it, and the direction in which he wishes to transform America is, to anyone whose views are not those of an aging boomer with tenure at some cow-college best known for its prowess in intramural agit-prop and the reek of stale bong-water, the wrong one.

Conclusion

☐   Obama

√   Romney

For the foregoing reasons, it is the opinion of Mr. Pyle as an American, and of Mr. Wemyss as an ally and admirer of America, that the only responsible choice is Governor Romney; and Mr. Pyle, an old Democrat himself of a dying breed, urges Americans to vote accordingly. Both candidates are, naturally, politicians; each has to some extent flipped, flopped, and fishtailed, and the extent to which this has represented legitimate changes of mind in Governor Romney's case is uncertain. (There is *no* uncertainty as regards President Obama's changes of position, almost all of which, from "gay marriage" to gun control, are simply reversions to the positions he always in fact held, held openly in the hothouse world of Chicago Leftist politics in the New Party days, and concealed only for tactical purposes in his national ascent. It is less dismaying, politicians being politicians, that he has chopped and changed, or that he has held the positions he holds, than that his first instinct is always and everywhere, when confronted with the possibility of not making the sale, to lie about it.) We cannot presume to say what are the relations between the soul of each man and his Maker.

We can however discern the obvious. Mr. Obama is not a believer in American exceptionalism. Most of the world is, which is why they as well as Americans expect more of America and hold it to a higher standard. Mr. Pyle is a believer in American exceptionalism. So is, in his way, Mr. Wemyss, who reminds all concerned that the United States is, after all, eligible for Commonwealth membership (and notes that the Commonwealth is wearisomely familiar with politicians of Mr. Obama's kidney). Mr. Obama's view is that Americans, as a sort of quaint foible, believe in American exceptionalism as "Greeks believe in Greek exceptionalism and the British believe in British exceptionalism." (For all his and his supporters' assertions to the contrary, Mr. Obama remains invincibly and irremediably provincial.) Well, Greeks can be proud of great predecessors from Pericles to Sophocles. And the nation of Smith and Mill, Newton and Brunel and Berners-Lee, Wellington and Nelson, Drake, Alfred, Milton, Shakespeare, Burns, Shaw, Thomas, and Churchill, needs yield place to none. But the United States is indeed exceptional. To be a Greek is a matter of blood and soil. To be or to become British is to give allegiance to the Crown, as a symbol, yes, of liberty, but one freighted with particular history. But anyone who assents to certain propositions —themselves, Mr. Wemyss insists, evolved by colonial Englishmen who created a country that is the legacy of Locke and the consequence of Coke and the common law —may become an American, whatever his birth, creed, ancestry, or skin tone. Governor Romney clearly believes this. President Obama....

President Obama does not believe in American exceptionalism; it appears, frankly, that the only exceptionalism in which he believes is the exceptionalism of Barack Obama. This is not simply a matter of his overreaching rhetoric or his failure to discourage, indeed his willingness to indulge, the really repellent cult of personality that his acolytes have created around him. It is, rather, implicit in his preference for rule by decree, his belief that a government with him in it should and can and ought to say when America has too much power, when Americans have made too much money, how far American's constitutional rights may extend, which Americans may be dealt summary execution from the skies without hearing or warrant, and how and to whom *he* shall redistribute power, money, right, and even life. For all we know, Governor Romney secretly sees himself in his deepest fantasies as such an arbiter of mankind; but we know perfectly well that Mr. Romney knows too much about basic economics not to know that this is a wild fantasy at best, and we know also that the press and both parties will not indulge Mr. Romney in any overstepping of bounds such as the press and the Democratic Party *do* indulge in Mr. Obama —the executive assassination by drone of American citizens without any process of law, let us say —acts that they would scream the house (and the Senate) down over if it were anyone else pulling that stunt time and again. That in itself is reason enough to boot Barack Obama, for the good of the country.

But of course the better reason is this: Governor Romney is willing to submit his plans to the judgment of the electorate and not simply run as if it's a tiresome ritual for one predestined to be the next face on Rushmore, and Governor Romney's plans clearly contemplate adherence to the law, respect for the Constitution, a foreign policy conducted in pursuance of American interests, and economic freedom leading to economic recovery. We have seen little of Mr. Obama's second-term plans; we *have* seen his — utterly deplorable —record; and the combination of those factors impels the conclusion that he dare not tell us what he intends next because it is at best no better than the complete pig's breakfast of the past four years, and quite likely a program that would send Americans into the streets with pitchforks, feathers, and tar.

That, surely, is enough.

Night of the Jackal: VV Putin & Ukraine:

2 March 2014, and ongoing

> *It is a regrettable fact that the habits inculcated in politicians who have successfully insulated themselves from criticism, challenge, and debate, lead them to folly: the potential folly of invading neighbouring states; the worse folly of failing to stand against such aggressions. Persons not steeped in defending liberties at home are weak as water in defending them abroad; and the cowardice, the cravenness, that moves politicians to support the demands of the professionally aggrieved at home for diminutions of liberty, leads inevitably to poltroonish truckling to tyrants abroad. Most significantly of all, an acceptance of the domestic claims to 'identity politics' – commonly advanced as a pretext for suppressing speech – leaves a leader ill-prepared to confront foreign aggressions predicated upon precisely that same claim.*

V V Putin —and it really is quite remarkably difficult not to write that as, 'Putain' — is not, personally or as leader of his kleptocratic, kakistocratic regime, bold by nature. Bullies and jackals are never bold: they crumble and scuttle when opposed with firmness. Vladimir Vladimirovich is not bold: he has *been emboldened.*

That he and his regime view Ukraine in the fashion in which the Pædophile Information Exchange viewed nine-year-olds, is no secret. That he has *acted* on his desires, has come as a surprise only to those who, after the manner of a Harman or a Hewitt in the 1970s, do not understand in what fashion predators are emboldened.

Blame can, in fact, be assigned.

Mr Wemyss, for one, warned, what time the House of Commons refused to back HM Government over Syria,[72] that the UK had entered thereby upon the future poetically foreseen by Larkin, in which the statues and war memorials looked *almost* the same, but the *numen* was fled. Ichabod: the glory has departed. And this was, and is, the more important because the government of the day in the United States was —and is — feckless and invertebrate. The spineless impotence of POTUS is a standing, and markedly unfunny, joke.

The invasion —and it is precisely that —of Ukraine by the regime and troops of the Mugabe of Moskva, is, as of this writing (2 March 2014), ongoing. And it is the direct consequence of Western weakness.

Let us consider, in this centenary year of the outbreak of the Great War, the echoes and overtones, and seek to find the theme in them.

Ukraine has, like Belgium a century prior, now called upon the other guaranteeing Powers to vindicate its integrity and sovereignty from a violation by one guaranteeing Power. No doubt, like Bethmann-Hollweg, Mr Putin regards these guarantees as 'a scrap of paper'; and like a later German chancellor, is no doubt already —as after the rape of Georgia — preparing a Reichstag rant for his puppet Duma in which he announces

---

[72] Mr Wemyss also stated at the time, quite clearly, that either had there been appalling mismanagement by the Government through the Usual Channels, or that Mr Miliband, as Leader of HM Loyal Opposition, had done something peculiarly terrible. It is acknowledged that Mr Miliband had been given, on Privy Council terms, access to the Government's intelligence and analyses. If he then reneged, for partisan political advantage, upon a commitment to back the Government, he ought to have been driven from his place and post, from any office of trust under the Crown, and from public life. This matter has never been satisfactorily resolved; and it is increasingly urgent that it be.

that this time, this really *was* his 'last territorial demand in Europe'....

It is quite true that Vlad the Invader's excuses — quite cynically threadbare ones which he hardly expects the world to believe — for committing acts that subject him to Nuremberg penalties, sound very like those of Hitler in the run-up to the Second World War: the assertion of a right of extraterritorial protection over ethnic Russians, Russophils, and Russophones in neighbouring countries, is naturally reminiscent of the Sudeten crisis; and the alleged 'provocations' , attributed to Ukrainians, advanced as a *casus belli,* are markedly evocative of Op HIMMLER and *Aktion Konserven,* the fake attack upon the German radio transmitter by alleged Poles in 1939. All the same, in 1914 the Tsarist entanglement in the Balkans, notably with Servia,[73] arose from decades of Pan-Slavism and the Tsarist Russian claim to be the protector, worldwide, of all Slavs and all Orthodox, wherever these might dwell; and the utter balls being talked by the Kremlin of Ukrainian 'provocations' and 'incursions' to justify invasion and war, follow with despicable fidelity the lying script of the 1914 Wilhelmstrasse of the Second German Reich.

Deplorably, also, the intelligence arms, foreign offices, and governments of the Western democracies, along with the *bien-pensant* press, the Beltway media in the US, and the Obama's Own Prætorian Press there,[74] failed utterly to anticipate the current crisis. Worse yet, they palliated the events that clearly signalled its imminence, not least by advancing once again the long-exploded claim that Russia 'would not do this because it would be economically unwise': the inanity maintained, fatally, by Norman Angell in

---

[73] The name was given an upgrade to the less servile-sounding 'Serbia' once that failed state became, accidentally, the Gallant Ally of France and the United Kingdom, in 1914.

[74] To the extent that these are not coterminous in any case.

and before 1914, which was disproved by the blood of millions. Millions whose blood had been wasted, in ponderable part, owing to Angell's diabolic theorem, that had paralysed thought and prevented the prevention of war.

The vegetative state of diplomacy in and before 1914 notably failed to take account of Vegetius' maxim, *Si vis pacem, para bellum*. Weakness, irresolution, and the failure to draw clear lines *and maintain them* – in fact, appeasement —was as much a feature of the years prior to 1914 as of those preceding 1939: and with the same result. That HM Government finds itself, in the centenary year of 1914, facing once again disunion (the attempt of a third-rate Tony Hancock impersonator to draw the Kinrick of Scots outwith the Union), austerity, retrenchment, and divided counsels, only to be confronted suddenly by the prospect of a European conflict, is simply appalling; and simply the result of its having forgotten the lessons of the past.

It was Barbara W Tuchman —no red-meat right-winger, she —who noted that a policy of drift, irresolution, and pussyfoot in international affairs did not keep, but rather positively jeopardised, the peace. History establishes this with its usual iron firmness.

Servia in 1914 was, unlike Ukraine, a failed state, and a state that was run as a private fiefdom by institutionalised terrorists, who, controlling military intelligence and the Staff, constituted —as the militarists in Japan in the 1930s constituted; as the ISI in Pakistan today constitute —an *imperium in imperio*. In the aftermath of the assassination of the Archduke at Sarajevo, Austria-Hungary was more nearly in the right than was Servia. The subsequent Balkan crisis could readily have been localised to the Balkans, as preceding Balkan crises had been in prior years, had HM Government been firm.

Colonel Alfred Redl had been the head of *k.u.k.* counter-intelligence in Vienna until shortly before the 1914 war. His opposite number in Russian service, then-Colonel Nikolai Batyushin,[75] ran him: for Redl, a closet case with a taste for high living and lots of dosh, was an arch-traitor who had delivered the entirety of Austria-Hungary's plans and dispositions, its orders of battle and all, to Moscow, and fed Vienna absurd underestimates of Russian military strength. When the *k.u.k.* forces, as Group B, marched on Belgrade, they were bloodied as a result, for Moscow had provided all Redl's intelligence to Servia. The parallels to the Snowden situation need hardly be underlined. *And nevertheless,* the 1914 war could have been localised —even had Russia yet intervened in support of Servia, and the French and Germans been drawn in in respective support of Russia and of Austria-Hungary —had HM Government been firm.

In 1914, Belgium's integrity, sovereignty, and neutrality was —similarly to Ukraine's integrity and sovereignty now —guaranteed by the Powers (including the Wilhelmine Reich). Even had the entire Continent been convulsed by a general war between the Entente and Central Powers, the war could have been prevented from becoming a *world* war had not Germany regarded this guarantee —of which, again, it was one of the guarantors —as a 'scrap of paper'. And once again, even had the entire Continent been convulsed by a general war between the Entente and Central Powers, the war could have been prevented from becoming a *world* war had HM Government in London made its position clear.

---

[75] Recently made the patron figure of the New Model KGB, the FSB, in place of Iron Feliks. *There's* a straw in the wind for you.

Simply put, the world's superpower in 1914, with a global reach and the backing of the Anglosphere it headed, which had kept and imposed a global peace for many generations, had it in its power at every step and stage on the road to a world war, to stop it or to localise it. In July 1914, had HM Government made it clear how far Vienna might go in dealing with Servia, the war could and should have been localised. Had HMG made it clear that Russian mobilisation should cause the United Kingdom and the British Empire to wash their hands of Moscow, France, if not Russia, should have acted so differently as to have stopped the spread of war. Had HMG made it clear that the first party to intervene in the Austro-Servian conflict should thereby cause Britain to side with the rival alliance, not even Berlin, in all likelihood, should have made a fatal misstep. And had HMG made it *clear* before, say, 1 August 1914 that any Power which violated Belgian neutrality thereby found itself in a state of war with the King-Emperor, it is difficult to imagine that even the Second Reich should have chanced its arm, gambling (as it did) that Britain should stay out.

Barack the First —to paraphrase Patrick Henry —may profit by that example.

This is an old story. The Peace of Amiens, and the antics of Charles James Fox and company, assured the resumption of the wars against Bonaparte. The failure to enforce the terms reached at Versailles and to reoccupy the Rhineland when challenged, made the Hitler War inevitable. Ms Glaspie's failure to speak clearly, led Saddam Hussein to invade Kuwait. To paraphrase the old maxim, If you wish war, embrace pacifism. Or as Mr Pyle puts it, In this world, until the Second Coming, those who beat their swords into ploughshares end up doing the ploughing for those who kept their swords.

In 1914, the Cabinet were deep in the toils of Irish Home Rule, had a precarious working majority owing only to Irish support, and knew that if the Government fell, Home Rule should fall with it. Accordingly, despite an abyssal division within the Liberal Party and the Cabinet, they felt — Squiffy in particular felt — it imperative to make any conceivable concessions to his internal opponents, to keep the party and the Government together. (The greatest threat to any Prime Minister —always —does not face him across the Despatch Box, but rather sits beside him on his Front Bench.) Sadly, the faction Asquith was determined to assuage was the 'peace at any price' set of Radical Liberals, supported by CP Scott and the *Manchester Guardian.*[76] The chances missed on 28 July 1914, for example, to stop or localise the war, were due wholly to the doomed attempt to keep on side the peace-at-any-price faction. In a very real sense, the proximate cause of the Great War's becoming what it was, the first *world* war, rests upon Morley and Runciman, Harcourt and Simon.

George Lansbury was a dear, sweet man, a patriot, a committed Christian, and an all-'round Good Egg. Cecil, with his 'Peace Ballot', was the same. They, and the Labour pacifists of the 1930s, crying for disarmament, unilateral if necessary, and the Tory appeasers of that decade, are —however barking Hitler was —directly and proximately responsible for the Second World War, all the same.

Tyrants and adventurers, bullies and jackals, must not be appeased, for that emboldens them. They must be opposed and quite firmly *and credibly* threatened with consequences if they set one foot out of line, and that line

---

[76] The more things change....

must be clearly drawn: for that gives them pause. More than that, it prevents them gambling, and provoking a situation in which the only available responses are war, or futile protests.

VV Putin has chanced his arm, and it *is* the fault of Mrs Clinton, and Mr Obama, and Mr Miliband, and Mr Farage for that matter, and many others, including Republicans in the US Congress and Conservative backbenchers in the House. It must now —and much more laboriously, and after blood has been shed —be cut off at the shoulder. The man and his regime must be stopped, now; and, if not deposed, rendered harmless by a Carthaginian peace.[77] (Russia is *not,* as it fancies itself, the 'Third Rome'; it is Carthage, Moloch and all. *Ergo, delenda est.*)

This does not yet mean war, and God forbid it ever should. It does mean extraordinary measures, requiring far more effort and money than should have been wanted to prevent the wretched situation's arising. It wants the addition of Mr Putin and his entire regime to the Magnitsky List; the cancelling of the G-8 summit; the expulsion of Russia from the G-8; the suspension of all trade and talks; the isolation, diplomatic and economic, of the regime; the freezing or forfeiture of the regime's assets and those of all who hold with it;[78] and, alas, as these things are porous, more. What that 'more' might be, it is not pleasant to say, not least because —not for the first time —it may mean making common cause with persons who, after the

---

[77] Mr Wemyss very much hopes than any terms imposed upon Putin include a requirement that he always henceforward wear a shirt in public. No one wishes to see the old wrinkly's decayed abs and sagging dugs. He is *not* a twilit werewolf of twenty summers, whatever he may think. (Although one does wonder, in light of his regular episodes of 'gay panic', if, in his boy service with the KGB, he wasn't sometimes a raven-who-swallowed, a rent-boy for the *Rodina.* It'd explain a good deal.)

(Mr Pyle observes that he has passed this footnote on the rather Lutheran principle that the best ways of dealing with the devil are to mock him; throw a pot of ink - or pixels - at the bastard; or, as here, both.)

[78] The deposed strongman of the Ukraine is said, by *The Times,* to have spent shocking amounts of dosh on lights and (how irremediably middle-class) fish-forks. Mr Wemyss cannot resist channelling Lord Jopling in observing that, Of *course* he was the sort who *bought* his furniture.

manner of the Taliban, then become the next threat with which we in the West must deal. Nevertheless, all options must now be on the table, from a new Stuxnet to arming the bloody Chechens; and all because a gang of fools encouraged the Putin regime, by the sheer supineness of 'reset buttons' and G-8 courtesies and appeasement, to try it on.

It had been so very easy to have avoided this. All it wanted was will and wisdom, firmness and attention to the immutable lessons of history. Alas, there are those who never learn —mostly on the Left —thereby dooming even those of us who have learnt, to repeat, bloodily, the old lesson. The gods of the copy-book headings, as Mr Kipling observed, are demanding and inexorable.

Conscience, Dishonour, and the Bishop of Buckingham
29 March 2014 - and since

> *If there is one lesson that must surely have impressed itself upon you in considering these ghastly facts and events, it is, That a* Stahl-treu *commitment to any political ideology which is intolerant of dissent and demands a* Gleichschaltung, *necessarily causes the committed to resort, sooner or later, to the politics of personal destruction, and to forfeit, in the end, his personal honour, his intellectual honesty, his conscience, and, ultimately, his soul.*

The reliably contemptible Alan Wilson, suffragan in the diocese of Oxford, has once more condescended to bestow his lofty wisdom upon the smocked peasantry in the pews. (As suffragan Bishop of Buckingham, he can —and dear God, does he —speak *ex cathedra* only from his accustomed throne in the *Grauniad* and, *urbi et orbi*, through gracious pronouncements to Fleet Street generally.) He has denounced other bishops as hypocrites and closet cases, and called —*Deus vult!* —for the crusading clerics of the C of E to 'creatively' defy, evade, and set aside the 'morally outrageous' strictures against same-sex marriage rites in the Established Church. These restrictions, he adds, with lordly disappointment, make him 'ashamed'.

Nice to know that *something* yet retains that power.

I am —as presumably the married Alan Wilson is not —a certified bit of old iron. I also happen to agree with Brian Sewell that civil unions are a good thing and same-sex marriage is a bad: although not for theological reasons, but because I actually understand the purpose of marriage as a legal institution.

(It exists for the orderly transmission of heritable property from two sets of in-laws who are reconciled to the marriage of their Precious Baby Girl to That Cad, or their Angel Lad to That Gold-Digging Little Minx [note to printer: 'Little Minx', not 'Little Mix' —although...], only by the prospect that the property in question is to descend to grandchildren who share their genes. Where property is commonly landed, marriage is between one man and one woman. Where —as on the steppes and in the deserts —it is divisible, consisting of jewels or gold or herds, polygamy is preferred. The one exception was always China, where a centralised bureaucracy and a suspicious emperor from very early times have promoted polygamy for two reasons: the conception of mass conscript pools, and the prevention of the accretion of latifundia the owners of which might then decide that the Mandate of Heaven had been transferred to *them*. (That after all is how emperors lose their thrones and warring states periods erupt: something no given Son of Heaven is eager to have happen to him.) It is notable that, for example, in the days of the khans, ultimogeniture was the rule, based quite reasonably on the odds that the elder sons should have had time and opportunity to do their own plundering before the Old Man managed to die in a raid, whilst the youngest might well not have done, and ought therefore to inherit the caput as his appanage. None of these cultures and their marriage laws owed anything to monotheistic theology. The only possible justification for the State's intervention in the arrangements of two —or more —lovers, and of the imposition of special burdens upon, and the grant of special privileges to, them, which make up marriage as a legal concept, is the State's interest in the orderly disposition of heritable property.)

But this —forgive me —is not the point.

It may well be that half the Bench of Bishops are buggers; or secretly run a drug ring trading Lovecraftian alien narcotics under the patronage of Cthulhu; or are cannibals; or are werewolves. (Oh, Christ. I've just inspired a new C of E fandom on LJ and at AO3, haven't I.) Presumably, as Alan Wilson is effectively begging the red-tops to try and 'out' bishops, he has some reason to believe what he claims to know. (Whether his actions are those of an honourable man ... well.) Personally, I don't care, for the purposes of this article at least. (The werewolf thing wouldn't bother me in any case. Phantomsby for Canterbury, says I!)

What repulses me specially here —an emotion with which I am all too familiar when Alan Wilson again slithers into my reluctant view —is his call for an insurrection, jacquerie, or trade action by the parish clergy.

It may be that there are times when conscience requires that priests defy their church. But if they are to do so, there is something they must do first: not as a matter of specially Christian ethics, but as a matter of elementary common morality regardless of whether one follows any faith whatever.

They must resign.

If you defy a three-line whip, you forfeit your place in the patronage system; you cease to be part of the payroll vote; you resign whatever offices you hold. I am not saying the C of E is or ought to be, or is or wants to be run like, a political party; I am saying that if even *politicians* can grasp this ABC of common morality, churchmen damned well ought to do.

No one cares particularly what Alan Wilson thinks or says, *quâ* Alan Wilson. (Not half.) He is solicited, importuned, and groomed —for soundbites, I mean —and occupies his gilt perch on the *Grauniad*'s *CiF* cage, not for his wisdom and insight and charity (not 'arf), but because he wears his collar the wrong way 'round and is allowed to wear purple bits and a pointy hat and a blinging pectoral cross if he likes. If he were the ~~bore~~ bloke down the local, no one'd ever have heard of him (what a wonderful world *that* should be).

In short, Alan Wilson's ability to display his conscience and to harangue the rest of us, rests solely upon his enjoyment of the place, position, and emoluments he enjoys by reason of being a bishop in the church he defies. And now he is calling upon others in the same situation to continue to enjoy the privileges and pay-packets of the C of E, such as they are, whilst openly defying its rules. Such as they are.

If you disagree with your employer's policy, and sabotage it, whilst still drawing your wages from that employer, and then bleat about how your conscience impelled you to do so, you are quite remarkably liable to be impeached by the question, What sort of conscience is it that has a chap stay on the books and take his pay whilst doing this?

This is not an issue of Christian morality, peculiar to that faith. This is a simple question of honourable dealing. Yes, it's true that public life in all walks thereof has nowadays more than its share of malignant moral midgets who expect the plums, the pay, the place, and the precedence of their positions, whilst refusing the burdens, duties, and traditions of 'em. Imagine, for example, were the First Commoner of the land, seated in the Speaker's Chair adorned by Denison and FitzRoy, by George Thomas and Betty Boothroyd and Jack Wetherill, such a man —or, rather, *don't*. Well: don't *imagine*. Nevertheless, this is not how honourable men, prelates or pagans, behave; and to attribute deceitful and dishonourable dealings to conscience merely magnifies the offence.

Any man can, by ill chance or ill judgement, fall into dishonourable courses. If he makes a (wait for it) habit of it, and calls upon others similarly to dishonour themselves, there comes a point at which one must ask if he is an honourable man and a gentleman.

Alan Wilson: if you are ashamed of the church that gives you your preferment, place, and pay, and which alone has afforded you a platform larger than a pub or a pew for your pronouncements, you have very few *honourable* courses before you: repent your views; refrain wholly from expressing them; or resign your posts. Which is it to be? Or shall it be dishonour?

'Come, Thomas! This isn't *Spain*...': Mozilla, Call-Me-Dave, and the Ghost of Orwell[79]
6 April 2014

> *And now the threads come together. Private demands for limits on speech slowly but surely infect the law; resort to litigation and lawfare to suppress speech opens the gate to laws which suppress speech; disrespect for liberty moves from assaults upon freedom of speech to assault upon families, and, in the end, to assaults upon free countries; and the mask comes off, revealing the true face of bestial hatred of the free, the poor, the dissenter, the democratic, and all who, intolerably, are not cowards and eunuchs of the same kidney as the opponents of liberty now unmasked.*

It has not been the best of months. Not personally: the Grand National was marred;[80] Mr Pyle is scrying worrisome omens even in the *winning* games of his hapless hometown Houston Astros, now reduced to play upon the Junior Circuit, and in his beloved Birds of Baltimore: even in their wins, and even thus early in the season; Mr Wemyss should prefer *not* to contemplate the state of England cricket; and Mr Pyle slipped, and fell, heavily and painfully,[81] in the mud and wet on his way to a party.[82] Only the Boat Race was an unalloyed pleasure in its result (and the

---

[79] For the love of God, *please* tell us you recognise that reference. Lie, if you must.

[80] The preceding races weren't all that one might have wished, either. Mr Wemyss takes the position that if one wishes to watch quadrupeds being raced in a desert sandstorm, one goes to camel races in the UAE, not to sodding Aintree.

[81] These things *will* happen – and hurt, rather – when one is built like Churchill. Not the PM: the *tank*.

[82] It was, he hastens to add, a *family* gathering, to which he was perforce invited. Of *course* no one

same again for the reserves and the women: an unfortunate year for the Tabs all 'round, really).

Much more pertinently, it has been a damned poor month for liberty.

An American journalist —for certain values of 'journalist' —has called for persons in public life who do not accept his views on anthropogenic global warming, to be gaoled. (He excuses those 'deniers' —that *useful* term that places those with whom he disagrees, on the moral level of people who pretend the *Shoah* never happened —who are *not* public persons, on the ground that they are fat morons from the *lumpenproletariat* incapable of reason or argument: which is what passes, nowadays, for a commitment to democracy and a love for the common man, on the Left.)

An ostensible coalition government in the UK, ostensibly led by ostensible Conservatives as its majority party, is contemplating legislation to allow actions to be taken against parents whose children complain that they are not being given enough cosseting or sweeties, thereby ensuring that the inner workings of the family shall be henceforth invigilated by the sort of jobsworths and jacks-in-office who stood by and allowed Baby P to be done to death.

Mozilla has sacked its co-founder, the creator of Java, Mr Brendan Eich, for having given, some years ago, a paltry donation to the 'wrong' side in a Californian political campaign:[83] the side in favour of amending that state's constitution so as to prevent judges from discovering in it a pretended right ('Look! It was there all along, hiding in the undergrowth!') requiring that marriage be redefined beyond the bounds of one man and one woman.

---

not impelled by a duty that cannot be evaded should invite him to a party otherwise.

[83] Thus causing cognitive dissonance in the Left, who insist that corporate bodies have no legal personality and mustn't have politics.

This, of course, was the side which, at the time, advocated precisely the view on whether there ought to be same-sex marriage,[84] as was advocated, at the time, by Barack Obama and Mrs Clinton. (The side supporting the expansion of the marriage right to persons of the same sex, was, by, contrast, the side upon which, then as now, Dick Cheney lined up.)

And of course, in the UK —under what is ostensibly a coalition government ostensibly led by ostensible Conservatives as its majority party —not only did the Act permitting marriages to be contracted between persons of the same sex[85] come into force, the mandarins and the EHRC published guidance which —in the teeth of governmental and ministerial representations to the contrary — not only threatens actions against tradesmen who chose not to enter into contracts to provide services to such weddings, *but also* provides that political and religious organisations which dissent from the new law may be barred from providing public services *and from ministering to their own flocks in NHS hospitals, HM Prisons, or any other publicly-funded setting or body.*

This differs from what is going forwards in Putin's Russia and in parts of Africa only in the *side* taken by the 'silencers' on one or another ticky-box on the list of Gay Topics. It is equally totalitarian and fascist.

Oh. We almost forgot. The Met sent rozzers 'round the newspaper in Croydon to threaten a journalist with being done for harassment for doing journalism on an admitted and convicted fraudster.

---

[84] So called. Nowadays, of course, it is insistently called 'marriage equality' or 'equal marriage' or some similar damned thing, a candy-floss phrase deployed, like 'denier', propagandistically, using emotive phrases that presume a certain conclusion in advance so as to choke off debate and darken counsel and avoid logical argument. Radek and Münzenberg should have been so proud of their lasting influence.

[85] The Marriage (Same Sex Couples) Act 2013 (c. 30).

It almost[86] makes one wonder why Vladimir Valdimirovich bothered with his Crimean *Anschluss,* when the West seems intent upon —if he'd only be patient —delivering itself into the hands of tyranny.

In fact, these alarming incidents are all much of the statutory and proverbial muchness, as we shall see.

We may begin by defining our terms —and even before that, laying our cards upon the table. As a partnership and individually, we long preferred Firefox; we have now switched to Opera. (IE is a perpetual Barmecide feast; Safari and Windows go together like kippers and jam; and Chrome is what happens when Microsoft cackles and rubs its hands and says, with Microsoftian hubris, 'No one can *ever* create a kludgier and more bloated browser than IE!' ... and Google sets its jaw, glares, and growls, 'Challenge accepted'.) We neither knew nor cared what the makers' politics were and are; we should have preferred to have been able to remain in happy ignorance of such otherwise immaterial matters.

Were one to ask Mr Pyle what his sexuality is —apparently this sort of intrusive query is now considered the height of delicate manners —his response ... well, all right, his *first* response'd be unprintable, alluding to the utter lack of its being your business; but his second should be, 'Moot and unsuccessful', on the ground that —even before he became old and fat and boring and failed —no woman, and indeed so far as he knows no man, and so far as he presumes no self-respecting *goat,* for that matter, should ever

---

[86] Only 'almost', mind. We know why Mr Put(a)in is in a hurry. His country is in an economic and demographic death-spiral which could be averted only by its being transformed into a land of free men, free minds, and free markets, and rejecting forever everything he, and his long line of Chekhist predecessors under tsar and commissar alike, represent. We exult in either outcome: we'd prefer a free and Classically Liberal Russia, but if the buggers *shan't* and *won't* reform, we'll happily toast their decline and fall.

have given him the time of day.[87]

Mr Wemyss, by contrast, is —although anything but camp —as gay as Christmas, and has never really made any pretence of being anything save a bit of old iron. He is after all not only a historian, but a novelist, whose lead characters include a gay couple and two bisexual men who have chosen to remain chaste (one being a devout Muslim and the other the Rector). And as a firm, Bapton Books will publish anything by anyone (so long as it's well-written), including a gay romance that's in the manuscript stage from one of our new writers.

Both Mr Wemyss and Mr Pyle support civil unions,[88] and have done for some time (Mr Pyle even in his lawyering days, not so much despite as *because* these undercut the Lawyers' Full Employment Act pursuant to which same-sex couples were mulcted of billable hours for matching wills plus powers of attorney plus this, that, and the other damned instrument).

Both Mr Pyle and Mr Wemyss are —like, Mr Wemyss points out, his fellow open gayer Brian Sewell — opposed to extending the *ius matrimonium* to same-sex couples: not, however, on religious, but rather on grounds of historical wisdom, legal principles, and political philosophy.[89]

Our interests having been declared, we turn to definitions. (It worked for the Greeks, after all: Socrates and that lot.)

Freedom of speech, expression, and publication is, as a legal and

---

[87] He is wont to say that he used, when younger, to swear that if he could find a woman who'd go out with him twice, and could bake cornbread, he'd marry her. Even after dropping the cornbread requirement – as neither Betty Crocker nor Martha White were really *suitable* – he failed to find a woman who'd go out with him twice. Or, commonly, once. The pool of women *now,* of course, who are at all interested in a short, stout, balding, boring, middle-aged military historian, is even smaller than it was when he still had remote hopes. He doubts it should be any better were he, improbably and pointlessly, to decide, in final desperation, to pursue men. Goats are right out.

[88] So long as these are decided to be enacted by the people or their democratic representatives and not imposed by judicial *diktat* or regulatory *ukase.*

[89] If the why and wherefore is *that* bloody important to you, turn to the annexe, then.

constitutional concept, a protection against a *government's* intrusion upon these rights (beyond laws against, for example, slander and libel). It is not applicable as such to commerce and personal interaction. (We as near as damn it said, 'personal intercourse', which should not, nowadays, quite have got our meaning across.) Thus, Mozilla, in sacking Mr Eich, did not mount an assault upon the *legal and constitutional rights* to freedom of speech, expression, and publication. The EHCR and HM Civil Service, by contrast, have done precisely that in their iniquitous and contemptible 'guidance'. So have the Metropolitan Police, by attempting to use laws against stalking and harassment to prevent an act of journalism's taking place. If any legislature in the civilised world were to enact legislation of the sort proposed by Mr Adam Weinstein, gaoling persons for holding and expressing contrary views upon global warming, that also should be an assault upon these freedoms.

Freedom of association, which necessarily implies the freedom *not* to associate with those whom one shouldn't care to meet in a lane, means simply that persons and organisations are free to choose their friends or members — and indeed employees. We accept the superiority of legal restrictions upon this freedom where it is abused by, say, racialists; we do not accept that it applies to legitimate differences of political opinion on issues of the day.

Employment at will, which is our preference, is the contrary both of the closed shop and of fixed-term contractual terms of employment, allowing employer and employee alike to sever the relationship as and when they so choose, for any reason or none. Again, we accept the superiority of legal restrictions upon this freedom where it is abused by, say, racialists; but not really otherwise.

Fascism, which George Orwell seventy years ago lamented was becoming simply a term meaning 'a different opinion to mine', has in fact a meaning (and not a rightist one). It is a policy programme of corporatism and cronyism based upon subscription to a governing ideology which must dominate all opinion, and which at best marginalises contrary opinion and ideology, both legally (as the EHCR are doing in the UK) and in private contract and public life (as Mozilla are doing); and which demands that there be no dissent, or that at best any dissent be punished by deprivation of livelihood and similar measures; and which extends its ideology, backed ultimately, if not always in its early stages, by the force of the State and of statute, into all areas of life, capturing, co-opting, and corrupting all organisations, including all parties, all unions and professional bodies, all corporations, all organs of the press, and all religious bodies, in the process of *Gleichschaltung.* You may observe it in its incipient form in the UK and the US, driven by the Left. As bloody usual. (Musso, after all, was a veteran Socialist.)

Thus, as Orwell always insisted, a **fascist** is not 'someone with whom I disagree and wish to abuse', but, rather, someone who supports ideological *Gleichschaltung.* So: Mozilla, Mr Weinstein, and the EHRC. (And quite likely elements of the unionised police at the Met: we've not forgotten Plebgate, you know.)[90]

Liberalism is a term stolen by Leftists to hide their true views and purposes. What it in fact means is a policy in support of free men, free

---

[90] Many of these no doubt do not believe themselves to be fascists, and believe themselves to hate and oppose fascism. They are fascists, objectively, all the same. They don't *realise* it simply because they are as thick as two short planks carved from coprolites deposited by ancestral *Suidæ* – that is, two short planks of fossilised pig-shit.

minds, and free markets, without fear or favour, privileges, corporatism, or cronyism. Mr Gladstone was a Liberal. Hayek (the economist, not the actress, although we know nothing of her personal politics) was a Liberal. *We* are Liberals. The Liberal Democrats in the main are neither (bar a few Orange-Bookers); the chairwoman of Mozilla and Mr Weinstein are profoundly illiberal; Mr Obama, like Mr Miliband, is a Leftist.

Diversity is a term deployed, as a shibboleth, by the Left, who mean by it 'a group of people visibly different to one another, who look good on a brochure, who meet quotas of representation for sex and ethnicity in a proportion at least equal to if not higher than the population, who come from superficially different backgrounds —religion included —prior to their all having gone to the same sort of school and having become similarly unchurched, and who may be relied upon to think the same damned thing about every damned topic: providing that they may vary in their opinions by each being further to the Left than the prior one'. In fact, **real diversity** means a group of people who, regardless of such accidental qualities, hold interestingly varied opinions, which they are capable of expressing cogently and logically, arguing for, defending, and changing if they are convinced to the contrary by logic and right reason.

Right, then.

As smocked, dung-spattered, straw-chewing peasants in the pews, we have been privileged to have heard the sermons the Bishop of Buckingham has graciously condescended to preach to us, from his suffragan demi-episcopal throne in the *Grauniad,* pronouncing *ex cathedra* that there are no Thought Police on the Left, there is no 'gay agenda', there is no 'Gaystapo'. His artificial lordship wants to pull the other one, there's a ring of six on it. (We say nothing against the man personally. Even though he has most recently called upon the parish clergy of the C of E to find ways around or openly to defy the Church's ban on solemnising same-sex marriages, and urged the outing of bishops he claims are engaged in long-term homosexual *affaires,* whilst continuing to enjoy his place, privileges, precedence, position, and pay-packet as a bishop of the Church of England. We merely note that Alan Wilson —who of course is pure as the driven snow himself —is engaging in actions which, unlike (of course) the suffragan bishop himself (Brutus is an honourable man), can be characterised as intellectually dishonest, mendacious, stupid, and dishonourable. When one's sole title to public attention comes from one's position in an organisation one is defying —and using that position to oppose —, most simple pagans, let alone Christians, tend to consider it the honourable course first to resign that position and to cease to be paid by the organisation one is seeking to undermine. You might very well think that the case here. We couldn't possibly comment.)

Now, if it was right for Mozilla to sack Mr Eich, it is also right —indeed, meet, right, and their bounden duty —that the C of E sack and for that matter unfrock Alan Wilson.

We don't think it necessary that you consult Paddy Power for the odds on that; and still less is it necessary to look out the odds against its being permitted by, for example, an employment tribunal or the EHRC.

Look here, damn it all. Had a for-profit corporation manufacturing durable goods of some sort said,

'Our new CEO has taken political positions, and some years ago gave to a campaign, representing views with which a little less than half the people in the country disagree. He continues to hold those views. We are gambling that the people baying for his blood can be appeased by our sacking him, and market research suggests that the backlash from the other side, if we *do* sack him, will do less damage to the bottom line than does keeping him.

'Therefore, as a business decision, without reference to the merits of his competence or to either position in the political dispute, we are, in pursuance of our profits and as fiduciaries for our shareholders, sacking him ...'

... well, they might have guessed wrong. The shareholders might have had a fit. But one could hardly judge such a board too harshly.

But of course that was not what happened with Mr Eich's 'resignation' (ahem). Mozilla instead took the position that it —an organisation that is quite tiresomely pious about its 'mission' to create an 'open web' —must let Mr Eich go on moral grounds.

Of *course* the silly buggers deserve mockery and boycotting.[91]

It's not merely that their hypocrisy —which they truly seem too thick to recognise — is at play. (Sacking Mr Eich is one thing. Lecturing and hectoring the rest of us, even whilst doing so, upon tolerance, the encouragement of open debate, and diversity of opinion? **Being lectured upon diversity and free expression by Mozilla is like being hectored about gun control by Leland Yee.**)[92]

When Mozilla not only surrendered to, but began enthusiastically collaborating with, a fascist tendency on the Left, they became —in Orwell's

---

[91] If one really wishes a combination of mockery, scathingness, and a boycott, we suggest Geoffrey Boycott.

[92] A California state senator and – until just recently – candidate for Secretary of State, noted for his anti-gun views and now under Federal indictment for attempted gun-running and bribery and all the fun of the fair. Of course, these are all merely allegations; the presumption of innocence attaches; and All That: you may take that as read.

formulation - 'objectively pro-fascist'. Look at what they have done, and how they have attempted to justify it.

On 3 April, the chairwoman of Mozilla posted to Mozilla's official blog.[93] What she said —and what we have to say about it, in square brackets, italicised —is as follows:

Brendan Eich Steps Down as Mozilla CEO

Mozilla prides itself on being held to a different standard and, this past week, we didn't live up to it. We know why people are hurt and angry,

[Not yet you don't. But you shall: read on. Or are we not 'people'?]

and they are right: it's because we haven't stayed true to ourselves.

We didn't act like you'd expect Mozilla to act. We didn't move fast enough to engage with people once the controversy started.

[Translation: We didn't surrender quickly enough.]

We're sorry.

[Indeed you are: sorry, pathetic, and contemptible.]

We must do better.

[And yet you are doing precisely the contrary.]

Brendan Eich has chosen to step down from his role as CEO.

[One does rather query this 'chosen' claim.]

He's made this decision for Mozilla and our community.

Mozilla believes both in equality and freedom of speech.

[Balls. Or, in American, horseshit. By its very actions, Mozilla has proven that not all opinions are equal and dissenting speech is penalised.]

Equality is necessary for meaningful speech. And you need free speech to fight for equality.

[That is neither the sole purpose nor the principle requiring freedom of expression: which is precisely not limited to speech that one or another group considers 'meaningful'.]

Figuring out how to stand for both at the same time can be hard.

[Evidently; and you lot cocked it up.]

Our organizational culture reflects diversity and inclusiveness.

[This is a simple and bald lie. Mozilla clearly does – and values – nothing of the sort: it penalises diversity of opinion and the inclusion of viewpoints at

---

[93] The subsequent attempts at spin, on 5 April, are simply not credible, particularly in light of the 3 April post.

odds with the orthodoxy of smuggery.]

We welcome contributions from everyone regardless of age, culture, ethnicity, gender, gender-identity, language, race, sexual orientation, geographical location and religious views.

[This is also a blatant lie. We rather doubt – although it is so immaterial that we cannot be arsed to look the matter out – that Mr Eich was motivated by religious views; but if he were – as many an observant Jew, obedient RC, committed Mormon, or faithful Muslim should be motivated by religious views to support the same side in the controversy as Mr Eich supported – such a person, by acting in accordance with his religious views, should be self-evidently unwelcome, and his contributions forbidden, by Mozilla.]

Mozilla supports equality for all.

[This is an obvious lie of Orwellian magnitude, unless 'all' is to be redefined as 'all who are bien-pensant'.]

We have employees with a wide diversity of views.

[And a shiny new chilling effect to prevent their daring to express them should those views not match those of the Grauniad. *If they decide to do so, well, then you've ex-employees who presumed to express a 'diverse' view, don't you.]*

Our culture of openness extends to encouraging staff and community to share their beliefs and opinions in public.

[This is a lie breathtaking in its scope and openness. Mr Eich did that, and look where he is now.]

This is meant to distinguish Mozilla from most organizations and hold us to a higher standard. But this time we failed to listen, to engage, and to be guided by our community.

While painful, the events of the last week show exactly why we need the web. So all of us can engage freely in the tough conversations we need to make the world better.

[Can this bloody woman be at all serious, or is this an extended piss-take? Try engaging freely in this conversation on any side save that of the Approved, and see how freely you can do so. It gets you fired from a company you co-founded.]

We need to put our focus back on protecting that Web. And doing so in a way that will make you proud to support Mozilla.

[Too sodding late for that. You're dead to us.]

What's next for Mozilla's leadership is still being discussed. We want to be open about where we are in deciding the future of the organization and will have more information next week. However, our mission will always be to make the Web more open so that humanity is stronger, more inclusive and more just: that's what it means to protect the open Web.

[Balls. Unless of course 'inclusivity' is to be defined as 'in agreement with the current conventional wisdom of a self-selected in-group'.]

     We will emerge from this with a renewed understanding and humility

[Sorry, did you say 'renewed'? Can't renew what you've clearly never possessed, and you damned well cannot do so by engaging in wilful misunderstanding and raw arrogance, the conviction that you are The Elect]

     — our large, global, and diverse community is what makes Mozilla special, and what will help us fulfill our mission.

['Diversity does not include diversity of opinion; offer not valid in most places; innumerable restrictions apply'....]

     We are stronger with you involved.

[Then weaken – and piss off. We're done with you.]

     Thank you for sticking with us.

[We're not.]

Mitchell Baker, Executive Chairwoman
[Note: We'd not have her as executive charwoman.]

[And now, the final bitterly-humorous irony, with our emphasis added. Had you been daft enough to have believed a word of La Baker's tissue of lies above: 'Mozilla believes both in equality and freedom of speech'; 'our culture of openness extends to encouraging staff and community to share their beliefs and opinions in public'; and all the rest of that sententious and lying twaddle: well, this must finally disabuse you of the idea that 'all of us can engage freely in the tough conversations we need':]

No responses yet
Comments are closed, but trackbacks are open.

The Mozilla logo is a dinosaur of some sort, so far as one can make out. We very much hope that this is an instance of unwitting prophecy; and that its fall —its deserved fall —is both imminent ... and, shall we say, meteoric.

Here's the thing. As a matter of general principle, we feel that a CEO —

or a bloke on the shop floor —ought to be subject to being sacked whenever the employer feels like sacking him (with the caveats we mentioned before). Even if it's for holding political views it's his right to hold, and even though those views are not illegal, immoral, or fattening. **When, however, the sacking is trumpeted as a triumph of principle, and accompanied by a lot of pi-jaw asserting that it vindicates the principles of 'equality and freedom of speech' and 'openness [which] extends to encouraging staff and community to share their beliefs and opinions in public', then the assertive trumpeter wants to have his trumpet shoved, assertively, up his arse.** It is not enough roundly to mock such people, particularly when they are making common cause with the objectively fascist; one must boycott them and do them the sort of economic damage they have chosen to mete out to those who resist the *Gleichschaltung*. After all, if Mozilla has the right to decline association with persons who hold Mr Eich's view on any subject at all, the rest of us, holding a sane view of Mozilla's behaviour (that sane view, by the way, being contempt and disgust), have the right to tell them to sod off, and to boycott their products.

But. Ah, but.... We are dealing with the objectively fascist here. 'Comments are closed', you see. In the US, they cannot —not yet —keep us from denouncing their actions, exposing them, and boycotting them. Not *yet*. And yet ... we mentioned this had been a bad month for liberty. Only a few days ago, Mr Justice Breyer marshalled three votes with his, against a five-vote majority,[94] in the Supreme Court of the United States, for a dissent that held that freedom of speech was a *collective* right, and must be for acceptable purposes.[95] Or as La Baker put it, 'meaningful speech', which is

---

[94] All right, a four-justice plurality opinion and a concurrence.
[95] *McCutcheon v Federal Election Commission*, 572 US __, ____ S.Ct. ____, __ L.Ed.2d __ (2014)

'free speech' so long as it 'fight[s] for "equality"'. And there are moves well afoot even in the US to penalise, by law, bakers and wedding photographers who decline the custom of a same-sex couple looking to marry.

The situation is of course worse in the UK. (Due largely to Ostensible Conservatives: Call-Me-Dave and his Wet, Islington, Notting Hill lot.) The House of Commons are evidently impotent to stop civil servants and a right-on, go-head quango from imposing the same penalties on the baker and the chap who takes the snaps; *and* **from denying the comforts of religion to the imprisoned or the dying if the minister of their faith represents a faith group that disagrees with the new Marriage Act.** The internal workings and interactions even of families shall now, if ministers get their way for the sake of having their tummies rubbed by quangos, be within the purview of the Nanny State, and this at the (cack-)hands of universally Leftist social services jobsworths (how long, do you think, before the first case is brought under the new 'Cinderella Law', if enacted, against parents who are deemed 'insufficiently supportive' of a not-strictly-heterosexual teen-aged child?);[96] and of course if even the Press dare ask an inconvenient question or press an inconvenient point, the Old Bill are now enthusiastically available to lean on them, with Leveson looming in the background.

In one sense, of course, this is actually rather encouraging. *Pace* Mr Obama, to slap the table and declare that a debate is over and no further argument shall be entertained, is not a sign of strength and confidence: it is

---

(Breyer, J, dissenting: 'a democratic order in which collective speech matters').

[96] Of *course* this would not be what Parliament meant by the proposed 'Cinderella law' (another classic sample of candy-floss language being used for propaganda, that). But it was mission creep that resulted in a law against stalking being used this week to threaten a journalist for committing journalism.

an indication that one feels oneself to be losing the argument, wherefore one must guillotine debate. (That it is a small step from guillotining debate to guillotining the debaters is, alas, too well-known to want emphasis. *Where they burn books, they will burn men.*)[97]

What La Baker, no doubt without having grasped it, and what Mr Weinstein quite unblushingly, seeks, is to have that same *Gleichschaltung* in America, to protect the Left against losing the debate. Sack the dissenters; *gaol* the dissenters; *silence the dissenters at all costs.* Totalitarianism naturally demands total submission.

It shan't work. It never has done. Another reason why VV Putin, like all Putinesque architects of the soul,[98] is in such a tearing hurry, is, The Anglosphere has a peculiar capacity for clawing itself back from the brink at the last possible moment, after a long stare over the precipice and into the abyss.

And there is this. Look again at the EHRC's idea that ministers of religious bodies which dissent from the recognition, *by* those faiths, of same-sex marriage, and which oppose the new Act, may and shall be banned from chaplaincies and hospital visits and prison ministries if a penny of public funds are used by those prisons and hospitals and care homes and orphanages and what not. Now, the C of E, as the Church by law established, may eventually bow to Rimmon —sorry, Parliament. And certainly one could find any number of vicars who'd enthusiastically take an oath of supremacy swearing themselves to the new order in any case. But

---

[97] Heine, *Almansor* : '*Das war ein Vorspiel nur, dort wo man Bücher verbrennt, verbrennt man auch am Ende Menschen.*' ('That was but a foretaste; where they burn books, they will in the end burn people also.') The writing is best remembered nowadays for its having been publicly burnt with the rest of Heine's works by the Nazis, and for the site of that outrage's having afterward been marked in memory thereof with these very lines.

[98] We apologise profusely, for that wretched pun, to Mr Pugin, the architect, in Heaven.

whatever their personal views, no Roman Catholic clergy can dissociate themselves from that communion's position —a *Magisterium* that is simply not going, foreseeably or indeed imaginably, to change —not and remain RC priests, they can't. There are schools of thought in Judaism whose rabbis cannot and shall not ever accept this. There are Nonconformist bodies that cannot and shall not ever accept this. And there is not a chance that Islam shall ever accept the new Act, or cease to oppose it.[99]

Contemplate, for a moment, quietly,[100] what is going to happen when the EHRC tells the Muslim and Roman Catholic populations of the United Kingdom that their imams and their priests are debarred from providing services and serving chaplaincies in HM Prisons and NHS hospitals.

The United States, of course, has no Established Church, as a constitutional matter. But the same Constitution equally forbids the passage of any law that precludes the free exercise of such religion as a citizen may profess; and that same Constitution provides against governmental interference with free speech. Imagine trying —as the Left seems bent upon trying —to silence speech there (and specially political and religious speech, which have extra protections in American constitutional jurisprudence) or to dictate to religious bodies what views they must hold to be allotted an equal space in the public square.[101] The political and legal firestorm should

---

[99] Honestly, *what* passes for thought in the Leftist mind, if you can call it that? They're forever banging on about the merits of Islam (which exist) and denying that there are any such things as Islamist radicals (which also exist), but when it comes to any conflict between their lily-white, metropolitan secular 'values' and pieties, and what Islam and a hell of a lot of other religions believe, they clamour to Take Up the White Man's Burden and lay down the law to the Peoples Without. When it comes to cultural imperialism and the Western Left, poor old Rudyard simply wasn't in it.

[100] Yes, that is precisely meant to be a Kiplingesque echo. Your Uncle Stalky is a Great Man.

[101] Mr Pyle can think of at least two acquaintances – formerly, *friends* – who precisely because of their obsessive, At All Costs, By Any Means Necessary support of same-sex marriage, want religious bodies silenced, and stripped of their tax status. Astonishingly, both are Jewish: which, when one considers just what religion it is that invariably becomes the first to hear the midnight knock upon the door, is incredible.

be visible from space.

Nor can all the police and all the social workers ever spawned successfully long suppress speech or plant little Stasi spies in Anglosphere homes, Cinderella or no.

And if La Baker hears of the consequences —as we very much hope she never must, for we very much hope they are averted: but if they are *not* – to Mozillists in, say, Malaysia, from her metropolitan Lefty, First World, privileged position and the reaction of your common or garden Islamist — Salafist to it ... well, Gruoch, that blood on your hands is *not* going to wash out.

Because let there be no mistake. *Gleichschaltung* is, always, the statement by one ideology that, *Thou shalt have no other gods.* It is always and everywhere an attack upon the individual conscience and upon all other bodies and allegiances, social, familial, religious, professional, fraternal, union, or other, that presume to claim a man's assent and loyalty. As was so for Sir Thomas More, one is not allowed to be silent, even when silence, legally, implies assent. As we noted in *'37: The year of portent,* 'it is not enough not to disagree. It is not enough to agree with reservations. It is not enough to agree without reservation. In the total state, in the totalitarian state, there must be unquestioned and unquestioning loyalty, and —thou shalt have no other Gods before the State': totalitarianism demands total, abject submission.

The fact remains: there is a shocking amount of objective fascism about, and Mr Weinstein, La Baker, the EHRC, the Coalition, and the Left who bayed for Mr Eichs' blood, are, objectively, fascists. *We repeat: these people are totalitarians. They are fascists.* And there is only one thing one can and must do when confronted with *that* lot.

Lawfully, by argument and by economic pressure, and by litigation if necessary,[102] one must defy them, reason them out of their follies, and strip them of any influence upon events.

One must resist.

---

[102] As long as we *are,* in the UK, stuck in the EU, we may as well get *some* use out of the damned thing and its overweening judges.

Annexe: Why we do not support extending the definition of marriage, as a legal concept, to two or more men, two or more women, or more than one each of a man and a woman:

Despite what Impressive Clergymen may tell you, mawwiage is not about twue wuv. Not as a legal institution, it damned well isn't. Nor is it religious. Every high civilisation —that is, every civilisation which has attained to a system of law —has had marriage. Only a fool should suggest that Periclean Athens, Republican and Imperial Rome, and Imperial China, say, crafted their marriage laws based upon the moral teachings of the Abrahamic religions —at least two of which these laws antedate.

And no civilisation has ever recognised marriage between two persons of the same sex.

There's a reason for that.

The legal institution of marriage is a contract between two persons (and, often, their families), to whom the State then grants extraordinary privileges and upon whom the State imposes extraordinarily onerous burdens and duties. Only a compelling State interest could possibly justify this intrusion into the lives of two or more people who happen to be romantically or sexually involved one with another.

As it happens, there *is* such a State interest, and it is rooted in the very purpose and meaning of marriage as a civil, legal institution.

Spouses become one another's intestate inheritors, principals, agents, fiduciaries, attorneys in fact, trustees, and beneficiaries. In some parts of the Anglosphere and the common law countries, they even now cannot be compelled to testify against one another. They are commonly awarded special tax status.

Why?

Marriage —as a civil, legal institution —is a device for the orderly disposition of heritable property. Full bloody stop. It exists and has always existed because there are two sets of mutually suspicious in-laws, each persuaded that their Golden Boy or Precious Angel Girl was entrapped and seduced by That Damned Gold-Digger or That Cad and Bounder, and each of whom are reconciled to the marriage only by the prospect that it shall produce grandchildren of their blood, who shall inherit from the prospective grandparents. That is why the spouses have special legal privileges and special legal duties —and why the law presumes that a marriage shall produce issue: so that the Gold-Digger and the Cad are constrained to preserve and augment the marital estate, including the portion inherited from the prospective grandparents, for the benefit, in trust, of the expected grandchildren.

These duties and privileges have no other justification; and they are so important that the State has always encouraged the contract that is marriage to be sanctified before the gods of the State, so as to impress upon the Cad and the Gold-Digger and all the community what an awful responsibility marriage is. But the marriage is not a rite or sacrament; only its solemnising is, in the same way that other special contracts are solemnised: a coronation, say, or the Blessing of the Regimental Colours.

Note that in Greece and Rome, marriage was always between one man and one woman. Note that on the steppe and in the desert, polygamy prevailed. This is telling. The purpose of marriage as a civil, legal institution is clearly reflected in this. Where landed property is the default inheritance, monogamy prevails. Where the property most likely to be inherited is personal and readily divisible: herds and flocks, gold, jewels, plunder (because no one is eager to inherit a hundred acres of sand or steppe): polygamy prevails. Similarly, European custom tends towards primogeniture, and indeed entail, historically: for keeping the land together is more important than being fair to younger sons. The Mongols in the days of Temujin, by contrast, practised ultimogeniture, whereby the family *caput* went to the youngest son: on the presumption that, by the time the Old Man got himself killed in a raid, the elder sons should have had time to carve out their own appanages by the sword.

The seeming exception to this, where a sedentary and landed people were encouraged to be polygamists, is China, and the polities that imitated China even when at war with China; and the reason there is likewise readily obvious. China has from a very early time had a centralised bureaucracy and, under whatever name, an Emperor. It is in want of manpower: large conscription classes for its traditional armies of mass. What the bureaucracy and the Emperor do *not* want is the creation of great landed fiefs: because this leads their possessors to decide that *they* are the choice of Heaven to be the Son of Heaven and to rule the Middle Kingdom, and that the Mandate of Heaven has been withdrawn from the current occupier of the Dragon

Throne. Warring States periods are fatal to former Emperors, and the bureaucracy finds them untidy. *Therefore,* the Emperors and bureaucrats have for ages said, *go forth, you black-haired millions of the Sons of Han, and take many wives and have many sons … and divide your property amongst them.*

It may therefore be seen by all who are not hermetically sealed of mind that, in not being satisfied with civil unions, the agitators for 'equal marriage' are simply demanding a set of legal privileges above other citizens, for which they cannot possibly have a justification, and without the corresponding duties; and all for the sake of their own feelings of self-worth, based upon what may be a passing and transient amour.[103] And to secure this, they have shown themselves willing to lie, to libel, to persecute, and to silence if possible any dissent.

Do you wonder that we despise these tactics —and are coming to despise the tacticians and their objectives as well?

---

[103] This of course also often brings the Cad and the Gold-Digger together for starters; but they can be shackled to their obligations by having children of their own blood, without always meaning to, and without going through the weeding-out processes of adoption.

Have another drink. You'll be in want of it.

E ven as this volume went to press, the threats continued to mount. Within the past month or so, a BBC programme dedicated to free speech and asking the knotty questions censored itself, and one of the audience invited to put questions for debate, because the question dealt with gay Muslims and the programme was being filmed in a conservative *masjid.*

Of course, in its services and its usual round of business, a mosque or a *mandir,* a *gurdwara* or a tin chapel, a synagogue or a cathedral, has every right to take its positions, preach its tenets, and decline to entertain heterodox views.

What such an institution has *not* the right to do —as no debating society or Union, legislature, or similar institution has not the right to do —is to host an ostensibly free debate for the whole of the public (and specially so when the debate is under the auspices of an organisation supported by ratepayers) and then to exercise a censor's veto.

In the past month, Mr Pyle, for example, has been told, on social media, by a Leftist, that to question the present US Administration is treason (the only crime actually *defined* in the US Constitution, and certainly not *thus* defined); he is old enough to remember when 'dissent was the highest form of patriotism'....

In the past *fortnight,* Brandeis University, in America, has withdrawn its invitation to speak, at its degree ceremony, to Ayaan Hirsi Ali, for the thought-crime of maintaining a feminist critique of Islam (and, specifically, of fundamentalist Islam). It has of course lied about the reasons, pretending that it had not been, when it issued the invitation, aware of the whole thrust of her work as a public figure: a claim no one can possibly believe, even if one credits its governors with a level of ignorance that should shame a seaside moke. In fact, and again *of course,* Brandeis bowed to a vocal minority of students and professors who hate free minds and free speech and any challenge to their views, and to an Islamic organisation that is objectively a pro-*Islamist* one.[104]

It is hardly necessary to point out that this intolerance is not a million miles removed from abject, pant-wetting cowardice; or that had the invited speaker been, say, Bettany Hughes[105] or Karen Armstrong, sought out to regale the luckless undergraduates with feminist denunciations of the Dead White Man in the Sky,[106] there should have been no move to 'disinvite' the speaker, or, if there had improbably been one, it shouldn't have been given a moment's consideration.

In the past *week,* a US Senator and a co-sponsor in the House of Representatives have proposed further restrictions upon 'hate speech', and

---

[104] They're not, in our judgement, merely in bed with the radicals. Indeed, Mr Wemyss submits, they're on their back, legs spread and knees at their lugholes, moaning, and gagging for it.

[105] And to think that she's the sister of a damned good cricketer and analyst. Breaks your heart, really.

[106] Cue the Norman Greenbaum track.

that the breadth of protected speech be further circumscribed and restricted: based precisely upon the very notions that motivated Mozilla's folly. And 'hate crimes' legislation remains popular with the interfering classes who think themselves elites, not despite it's creating specially protected classes, but precisely because it does, thereby striking at the very heart of the concept of equal justice under law. The sort of people who bang on incessantly about the evils of 'privilege' are the most assiduous in seeking to promote it, and to infect the law with it. All politicians are apes, of course; but they are sedulous apes: sedulous of the culture, and never more so than now. If there were not, in a few elements of the Right and almost all of the Left, a driving urge to suppress dissent, lest argument be required and perhaps lost, by means including lawfare and the attempt to deny gainful employment to persons who do not register Approved Views, no politician in a democracy —not even Dingy Harry Reid, the Dim Bulb from Searchlight —should be setting up opponents as foci of a Two Minutes' Hate and seeking overtly to diminish free speech *by law.* The law is being made to follow a decadent culture into its own decay.

The fact is stark, and simple. The threats to freedom —of speech, but not of speech alone —continue, and continue to grow. They begin in private discourse, where they are not themselves a *legal* threat; but they metastasise. The next step is to invoke the law to prosecute an opponent, to close off debate; or to punish an opponent with vexatious and frivolous litigation. The machinery of the State becomes involved: tax agencies mobilised against ideological opponents; harassment and stalking laws brandished against journalists; civil rights laws perverted, through mission creep, to pursue merchants *and religious institutions* who choose not to provide services to one or another group. (In a despicable irony, the State then declares that dissenting religions may not provide services to their own congregants in any place the State gives tuppence to.) Then the legislation begins, limiting a right here, denying a freedom there.

Until the final moment when the dissenters can be hounded from public life and private employment, silenced, gaoled, 're-educated', killed, there must be some façade, some scaffolding, some false-front erected to give an air of verisimilitude to the otherwise bald and unconvincing narrative of the suppression of rights and of dissent. This is found in resorting to 'identity politics'.

We don't wish to be complete Kants about this,[107] but: if a universal right ceases to be universal, it ceases to be a right. Or, rather, it has ceased to be *recognised* and honoured and observed as the right it inherently and absolutely and inalienably is and remains. When a hierarchy of who may and who may not claim a universal right is erected, what exists is no longer a recognised body of rights, but a series of privileges which are doled out by the State to its cronies or those whom it chooses to indulge or fears to provoke. But in a free society, those who, as the hired servants of the people, act as the State, must be made to fear to provoke the people as a whole: that is the definition of democracy.

And when the governors no longer fear or need even hear the governed, when they have suppressed all dissent and challenge and heed only their courtiers and lickspittles, they lead the governed into folly and danger; and their follies and their despising of liberty do not stop at home, but begin to

---

[107] Sorry. We swiped that, in a roundabout way, from Professor Morgenbesser.

drive foreign affairs, foreign policy, and foreign adventurism. 'Hard' tyrants, under these circumstances, chance their arms; and 'soft' tyrants, who never set out to be tyrants but have been made decadent by the silence of criticism and dissent at home, find themselves —particularly when the hard tyrant has advanced as his justification the principle the soft tyrant has accepted at home, of special privileges attaching to ethnic or religious or other identity —flaccid as maggots, incapable of muscular response; and thus invoke the conflict they had sought to flee.

The stark fact is, This must stop. And the stark fact is, It is not going to stop on its own. And the stark fact is, It must *be* stopped, and we must stop it.

If you happen to be gay, or to be —regardless of your own interests or sexuality —a supporter of extending the right to marry to same-sex couples, you *must,* if you are an honourable person, stand up for the right of others to dissent without punishment, without fear or favour. If you advocate *not* extending the *ius matrimonium* to same-sex couples, you must embrace debate, and stand with those with whom you disagree, in support of the principle that speech must be free and debate open and vigorous and un-policed. If you are a fundamentalist member of any religion —Judaism, Islam, Christianity, Dawkinsian[108] secularism —you are morally obliged to stand up for all your philosophical and religious and irreligious and ideological opponents.

If you do not believe in free speech and free discourse —free of private as well as of public threats: for who is monstered today is all too likely to be

---

[108] An appropriate portmanteau word, combining 'Dickensian' and 'mawkish'.

prosecuted in the end, as Heine might have said —say so, God damn you. Do not take refuge in fairy-floss, with caveats and cotton-wool words, with damned-fool mantras such as your 'Yes, but' and 'tolerance cannot tolerate intolerance' and 'hate speech is not protected speech' slogans that take the place of rational thought and are used, as squid use ink to cover their retreats, to end and evade argument.

If you do believe in free speech, you must believe in it as the *universal* right it is. You must support it in your fiercest enemies as in your friends. For if you do not, you prove yourself no true believer in it.

As a matter of common honesty, let alone intellectual honesty, if you belong to a group or take the penny of an organisation which has a view to which you are wholly opposed, *and which exists to express that view,* you must first resign before you then condemn your (by then, *former*) colleagues or employers. If you resign the whip, after all, you must leave the front bench, and indeed the party on whose platform you stood and whose patronage got your bum on the bench. If, however, you are in charge of a group or organisation which does *not* exist to put a view, and to whose legitimate functions such matters are indifferent, you must not discharge people because their politics are not your own, and they have dared express them. This is the difference between a commercial firm and the Church of England. (If you belong to a group or organisation which ought by rights to be indifferent to specific political positions, but which clamantly proclaims itself a champion of free speech on all such positions —free as against both private and public suppression, mind you —and you then sack people for speaking freely upon specific political positions that are 'things indifferent' to your purpose, you are so contemptible that you almost certainly hold a management post at Mozilla.)

Where they burn books, they'll eventually burn writers and readers and all manner and condition of people. And, in the same fashion, where the heckler's and lobbyist's and the terrorist's and the fundamentalist's veto is allowed to silence speech in the private sphere, whether by threats of violence or by more insidious means, then, by the irresistible logic of *Gleichschaltung,* speech shall soon enough be silenced or suppressed by public and governmental pressure.

Whilst we have the freedom to speak out, we must all of us do so, condemning all who would restrict that right whether privately or by prosecution, lest we lose that freedom. Or in plain and pungent Texan from Mr Pyle, 'You have a voice. You want to keep it, just you call the sons of bitches out, every time'.

Colophon

Headers and subheaders are set in IM Fell type variants; the text, in EB Garamond.

www.ingramcontent.com/pod-product-compliance
Lightning Source LLC
Chambersburg PA
CBHW070424290526
45791CB00005B/1823